JULIAN HAWTHORNE

Incredible Mysteries: Internet Mysteries

Contents

Introduction

I n the boundless expanse of the internet, a domain where knowledge is infinite and connections are endless, there exists a parallel world veiled in mystery and steeped in intrigue. This digital landscape is a haven for unanswered questions that echo through forums, for enigmatic figures who vanish as swiftly as they emerge, and for tales so bizarre and complex they straddle the line between fiction and reality. These stories, unfolding in the hidden crevices of cyberspace, beckon us on an expedition to unearth truths buried deep within layers of digital enigma.

The internet transcends its functional role of information and interaction; it has evolved into a bastion of unsolved mysteries, a canvas painted with the brushstrokes of the unexplained and the inexplicable.

As we embark on this exploratory journey, we delve into narratives that have captivated and intrigued millions. From the perplexing evolution of an ordinary YouTube channel into a complex, maze-like puzzle, to the bizarre vanishing of a well-known online entity leaving behind a trail of cryptic messages and speculative theories. These stories blur the boundaries of the virtual world, impacting lives, igniting debates, and challenging our perception of reality.

What is the catalyst for these mysteries? Is it the veil of anonymity that the digital world provides, the inherent human desire to impose order on chaos, or the seductive lure of the unknown? Navigating through these mysterious narratives, we encounter the human element behind the screen — the originators, the explorers, the believers, and the skeptics.

This exploration is more than a mere collection of internet mysteries. It represents an in-depth examination of the human psyche in the era of digital dominance. It stands as a testament to our relentless pursuit of answers and our innate fascination with that which remains elusive and unexplained. We invite you to partake in this quest, to plunge into the depths of the internet's most compelling mysteries, and to reflect on the questions they pose about technology, humanity, and the vast, uncharted expanse of the online universe.

Prepare to be captivated, confounded, and perhaps even disturbed as we embark on this odyssey. The journey ahead is riddled with twists and turns, interweaving facts with fiction, and presenting stories that challenge our understanding of what is real and what is possible. Welcome to the enigmatic world of the internet, a realm where the whispers of the unknown resonate long after the screen fades to black.

In this digital odyssey, we will encounter unsolved puzzles that have baffled the brightest minds, witness the rise and fall of online communities shrouded in secrecy, and explore the dark corners of the web where the most tantalizing of mysteries reside. We will meet individuals who have dedicated their lives to unraveling these digital enigmas, and others who have found themselves unwittingly entangled in web-based riddles with real-world consequences.

Through these pages, we will traverse a landscape where reality is often more strange than fiction, where digital footprints lead to unexpected destinations, and where the quest for truth takes on a new dimension. In this world, a single piece of code, a fleeting image, or a cryptic message can unlock doors to hidden truths and new realities.

So, let us step into this uncharted territory together, with eyes wide open and minds ready to question and to learn. The mysteries of the internet await, each a puzzle piece in the grand tapestry of our digital age. As we journey through this labyrinth of secrets and revelations, we may find that the answers we seek are not just about the mysteries themselves, but also about ourselves, our society, and the ever-evolving relationship between humans and the technology they create.

Embark on this journey with a sense of wonder and a willingness to embrace the unknown. The stories you are about to discover are as varied as they are intriguing, each a unique reflection of the vast and mysterious digital world we navigate every day. Welcome to a journey into the heart of internet mysteries, where each discovery brings new questions, and where the search for answers is an adventure in itself.

11B-X-1371

I n 2015, a mysterious and chilling video titled "11B-X-1371" surfaced on the internet, sending waves of intrigue and fear across the globe. Initially brought to public attention by the Swedish tech blog GadgetZZ.com, this eerie black-and-white footage, lasting two minutes, features a sinister figure donned in a plague doctor costume. This haunting character meanders and stands in the ruins of an abandoned building, with glimpses of a desolate forest seen through the remnants of windows.

The video's spine-tingling atmosphere is amplified by a disturbing soundtrack of jarring, dissonant buzzing noises. Adding to the enigma, the masked figure ominously displays a hand with a light that blinks in a cryptic, irregular pattern. Mysteriously, the film offers no credits or hint of authorship.

Hidden within this perplexing video and its sound spectrogram are messages encoded in various ciphers and encryption systems, alongside harrowing images linked to infamous murder cases, including the Boston Strangler. These cryptic messages and images have led to rampant speculation and theories, ranging from warnings of bioterrorism against the United States to the possibility of it being an elaborate hoax, a viral marketing campaign, or even a student film project.

The intrigue deepened when it was revealed that the video had actually been uploaded to YouTube months before it gained notoriety, accompanied by a similarly ominous binary code message. The uploader, known only as AETBX, hinted at discrepancies in GadgetZZ's account of how they obtained the video. Internet sleuths later pinpointed the filming location to the haunting Zofiówka Sanatorium in Poland, dating it between November 2013 and its eventual release.

In a dramatic turn, three months after the video first caused a global stir, an individual named Parker Warner Wright came forward claiming to be the creator. He described the video to The Daily Dot as an art project and even released a sequel, "11B-3-1369," challenging viewers to replicate his plague doctor mask as proof of his claim. This revelation only added more layers to the already deepening mystery of "11B-X-1371."

The video opens with a tense and mysterious scene, the camera trembling as it captures a shadowy figure lurking between two large openings in a brick wall. Through these gaps, the rustling leaves of trees sway in the wind, creating an unsettling backdrop. This eerie visual is underscored by a soundtrack filled with obscure electronic buzzes and hisses. The enigmatic figure gestures cryptically with their right hand, first showing three fingers, then one, and finally two.

Shrouded in darkness, the figure strikes an ominous pose, arms cloaked and outstretched, as the camera retreats and orbits slowly to the right. A sudden jump cut shifts the scene, illuminating the figure and revealing their attire: a sinister plague doctor costume. This includes a long, dark hooded cloak and a mask with a long, beak-like protrusion, completing the foreboding ensemble. The figure raises their right hand, palm outward at shoulder level, displaying a mysteriously blinking light in its center. This blinking is synchronized with the soundtrack's beeping tones.

The narrative tension builds as the figure, now motionless, turns their head to contemplate the blinking hand. Outside, the once animated leaves have stilled. The figure's gaze shifts from the hand to the camera, which has now steadied, creating a brief, intense connection with the viewer. A rapid series of jump cuts follows, with the figure alternating their gaze between the hand and the camera, culminating in a pointed gesture directly at the lens.

In a swift transition, the costumed character reappears, hands at its sides, facing the camera. A sequence of jump cuts captures the figure turning right and then back again, adding to the suspense. The figure then pauses, turns its head slowly to the left, and looks down at a box marked with various triangular sections. As the image briefly fragments, the figure glances to the right. For the remainder of the video, the cloaked figure remains motionless, back against the wall. The camera, seemingly handheld once again, occasionally doubles the image with fleeting video effects, leaving the viewer in a state of haunting uncertainty.

On October 12, 2015, an intriguing mystery landed on the doorstep of John-Erik "Johny" Krahbichler, the founder of the Swedish tech blog GadgetZZ. He received a perplexing package in the mail, postmarked from Warsaw, addressed to "Johny K." at the blog's Helsingborg P.O. box, with no return address. Inside was an unassuming DVD, marked with a lengthy alphanumeric string that piqued his curiosity – initially mistaken for a product key.

Believing it to be software for review, Krahbichler decided to test it on a spare laptop. To his surprise, he didn't find software but a bizarre and unsettling video. He admitted to The Washington Post that the video's odd nature left him confused and intrigued. It was upon closer inspection that he began to uncover the myriad of codes and hidden letters scattered throughout the video.

Krahbichler's initial attempts to unravel the mystery proved fruitless, prompting him to share his experience on his blog, complete with images of the disc and envelope. The story quickly caught the attention of the media, with Gizmodo covering the discovery shortly after. Lily Hay Newman from Slate commented on the video, describing the experience of watching it as akin to the eerie and disconcerting feeling of viewing the cursed videotape from the horror film "The Ring" released in 2002.

The enigma of the "11B-X-1371" video deepened with the revelation that Johny Krahbichler wasn't the first to bring it to public attention. Investigations revealed that a YouTube account named "AETBX" had uploaded the video in May, the only activity on the account. Accompanying the video was a mysterious binary code, sparking curiosity among viewers. AETBX, surprised by the sudden surge of interest in a video posted months ago, engaged with commenters, who speculated that he might be the creator – a claim he strongly denied.

The plot thickened when The Washington Post reached out to "Daniel from Spain," the person behind AETBX. He claimed to have also received the video unexpectedly, sent by an unknown girl who allegedly found it on a park bench. This twist was compounded by an update from Krahbichler, who noted that the video had surfaced even earlier on a paranormal board on 4chan, further muddling the origins.

Further leads appeared but quickly unraveled. Triton TV, a student film group at UC San Diego, briefly emerged as a potential source when a screenshot of the video appeared on their blog with a cryptic binary title. However, the group clarified that their site had been hacked, and the image was likely posted by the hacker. Another false trail emerged with Parker J. Wright, who responded to a Twitter inquiry clarifying he wasn't the Parker Wright who posted the video on YouTube with a cryptic message.

While the creator's identity remained shrouded in mystery, the video's filming location was pinpointed. A Polish internet user, following the unfolding story, visited the Zofiówka Sanatorium near Otwock, just south of Warsaw. The sanatorium's distinctive windows and graffiti matched those in the video, dating its creation between November 2013 and April 2015, based on comparisons with earlier photographs of the location. This discovery added a tangible, yet eerie, dimension to the ongoing puzzle of the video's origin and purpose.

In the wake of the initial frenzy surrounding the mysterious video, a new chapter unfolded in late November when a Twitter account named Parker Warner Wright emerged. The account's owner staked a claim to the video's creation, joining a chorus of others on the internet who had made similar assertions. As 2015 drew to a close, various individuals attempted to authenticate their claims by posting their own videos.

At the month's end, Wright stirred anticipation by announcing the release of a new video, "11B-3-1369," on his YouTube channel, scheduled for release in "1.444 metric hours." True to his word, the video appeared, featuring the now-iconic plague doctor figure. This sequel, set both in a forest and inside the sanatorium, was quieter, with an eerie soundtrack and synchronized electronic tones mirroring the blinking light on the figure's hand. Notably, the plague doctor was joined by a woman in a white dress, her face obscured by bandages.

Weeks later, The Daily Dot published an interview with Wright, where he revealed himself as a U.S. citizen residing in Poland. He described the videos as an art project, stating he had distributed three copies in May 2015 – two in public spaces in Poland and one via 4chan. This interview suggested that YouTube user AETBX was not involved in the video's creation. To lend credibility to his claim, Wright issued a challenge on his Facebook page, inviting people to replicate the plague doctor mask, which he claimed to have designed and built.

Skepticism lingered among some of Wright's Facebook followers, who noted discrepancies in the costume between the two videos. Wright attributed these changes to his desire for an improved cloak in the second video. Krahbichler, the GadgetZZ founder, eventually endorsed Wright's claim, reasoning that the intricacies and duration of Wright's involvement made it unlikely to be a mere ruse. Further adding to the intrigue, Wright revealed in a Facebook exchange that he had chosen Krahbichler as the recipient of the video due to a chance encounter where Krahbichler had given him a business card, presumably at a tech event. This revelation provided a plausible link between the mysterious creator and the tech blogger, deepening the enigma surrounding the entire affair.

After Johny Krahbichler's blog post about the mysterious video, the Reddit community dove into deciphering its hidden messages. They uncovered numerous cryptic elements, including an encoded title "11B-X-1371," which became the de facto name of the video. International Business Times' James Billington noted a disturbing aspect of the video's audio - some heard a phrase like "I would love to kill you" repeated throughout.

The intrigue deepened when a user analyzed the audio's spectrogram, revealing hidden text and images. Among the text was a chilling plaintext message, "You Are Already Dead," while other parts remained encoded. The images were particularly alarming, depicting scenes of mutilation and torture. However, fears of a connection to a serial killer were alleviated when it was discovered that the images were sourced from horror films like "The Bunny Game" and "Slasher," as well as an infamous photo of a Boston Strangler victim.

Most of the video's messages carried an ominous tone. A spectrogram of the DVD's menu revealed a skull image and more codes. The binary title in AETBX's YouTube post translated to "Muerte" (Spanish for "death"), and the description ominously warned "Te queda 1 año menos" ("you have one less year" in English). A cryptic triangle-and-square message in the video was deciphered as "Ad oppugnare homines" in Pigpen cipher, Latin for "To attack or target men."

The video's use of a plague doctor costume spurred theories linking its threats to bioterrorism. One plaintext message warned, "The eagle=infected will spread his disease. We are the antivirus will protect the world body," while another message ominously stated, "Strike an arrow through the heart of the eagle." Additionally, the year 1371, featured in the video's title, was noted to coincide with the period of the Black Death's devastation in Europe, adding a historical dimension to the video's unsettling narrative.

The meticulous analysis of the "11B-X-1371" video by the online community unearthed even more cryptic elements, including Morse code and various texts encoded in common ciphers. A striking discovery was the Morse code translating to "RED LIPS LIKE TENTH." Furthermore, a sequence of coordinates was identified, pointing to the latitude and longitude of the White House in Washington, D.C. This led to a disturbing interpretation of the "RED LIPS" phrase as a possible anagram for "KILL THE PRESIDENT," perceived by some as a threat against the United States and then-President Barack Obama.

Another deciphered message from the video read, "STANDANDFIGHTWITH USTAKEDOWNTHEBLACKBEASTKILLHISDISEASEORFALLWITHTHEREST." Johny Krahbichler, who initially brought attention to the video, speculated that the term "BLACKBEAST" could be a reference to President Obama. Despite these potential political connotations, Krahbichler did not believe the video represented a terrorist threat, but rather carried a political message.

The mystery deepened when the individual identifying as Parker Warner Wright, the alleged creator of the video, appeared on Twitter. In late November, Wright addressed those dedicated to decoding the video, suggesting that they were still far from grasping its true message. He hinted that the video's codes were designed to be a collaborative puzzle, noting that "Not one individual could decipher the whole," emphasizing the complexity and intended community effort behind understanding the video's cryptic content.

The video, with its enigmatic and menacing message, sparked widespread speculation about its purpose. Released shortly before Halloween, some thought it might be a seasonal internet hoax. Krahbichler, initially alarmed by the decoded threats, later considered it an elaborate joke, noting that anyone who knew him personally would realize his lack of expertise in deciphering such messages.

Another popular theory was that the video served as viral marketing for an upcoming film or video game. This idea gained traction when a Redditor pointed out the similarities to Dan Brown's novel "Inferno," which was being adapted into a film. The novel features a wealthy antagonist who creates a threatening video while wearing a plague doctor costume, an imagery echoed in the mysterious video.

The speculation extended to the possibility of the video promoting the new season of the Syfy series "12 Monkeys," inspired by the Terry Gilliam film. The series, involving time travel to prevent a catastrophic epidemic, frequently uses the phrase "You are already dead" and features a plague doctor costume. A Redditor suggested that the hand signal "3-1-2" in the video could hint at the show's third season.

Lastly, the video's Polish origins led some to believe it was a low-budget marketing tactic by emerging video game studios in Poland, recalling a similar viral video from years prior that had parodied a children's show. However, the production quality of the 11B-X-1371 video seemed to differ from that of the earlier Polish video.

It seemed improbable that established media entities, like those behind "Inferno" and "12 Monkeys," would engage in marketing tactics involving disturbing images and implied threats against a U.S. president, due to the potential for adverse publicity.

An alternate hypothesis linked the video to electronic musician Skrillex. Coinciding with the video's internet debut, Skrillex released a song titled "Red Lips" and later tweeted the song's title repeatedly. This led to speculation that the video might be a cryptic promotion for his music, especially since other artists in the genre have used spectrograms to conceal images. This theory was bolstered by Skrillex's claim of having unreleased work stolen from his hotel room. However, Krahbichler pointed out that the connections to the advertised works were tenuous.

Parker Warner Wright, believed by Krahbichler and The Daily Dot to be the video's creator, described the video and its sequel as the beginning of a series of art projects. He remained vague about their themes, likening his work to ocean waves, open to different interpretations and interactions. He expressed a commitment to continue his art series, driven by internal motivation rather than public demand.

Wright posted a new video titled 110A30213 on his Facebook page shortly before the 2016 U.S. presidential election. In this video, Wright appears as a military officer or dictator addressing a crowd. Krahbichler speculated that this politically charged video could be related to the election, noting the significance of its release date in relation to Guy Fawkes' famous quote "Remember, remember, the 5th of November".

Cicada 3301

D ive into the digital labyrinth of Cicada 3301, a cryptic phenomenon that has enthralled the internet's collective mind since its mysterious emergence in 2012. This enigma, emerging from the shadowy depths of cyberspace, has sparked a global frenzy of codebreakers, cryptanalysts, and digital detectives. The allure of Cicada 3301 lies in its complex tapestry of codes, symbols, and intellectual challenges, making it one of the most enigmatic and enthralling online puzzles of our time. It's not just a puzzle; it's a gateway to an exclusive and enigmatic circle, weaving a legend into the digital age.

The saga of Cicada 3301 is a distinctive and captivating narrative in the annals of internet history, symbolizing the limitless possibilities of online collaboration and the magnetic charm of intellectual quests. While the true essence of its mysteries remains shrouded, the legacy of Cicada 3301 continues to echo, standing as a monumental tribute to the uncharted mysteries of the digital universe, beckoning the curious and the audacious to unravel its secrets.

On January 4, 2012, an enigmatic post appeared on 4chan, authored by "3301": "Hello. We seek the exceptionally bright. A test has been crafted to discover such individuals. A concealed message lies within this image. Unearth it, and embark on a journey towards us. We eagerly anticipate meeting those who prevail. Good fortune."

Intrigued users swiftly uncovered that the image, when viewed as a text file, divulged a cascade of text, within which a decipherable cipher hid. This cipher directed seekers to an Imgur link, displaying a misleading solution image. Further exploration of the original image unearthed a book code and a subreddit link, holding more clues.

Decoders employing the book code extracted a phone number. Upon dialing, they received a cryptic commendation: "Excellent work. The original .JPG image is tied to three prime numbers, 3301 being one. Locate the others, multiply them, and append '.com' to discover the next phase. Farewell."

The puzzle deepened when solvers realized the additional prime numbers were the dimensions of the initial 3301 image shared on 4chan: 509 and 503. Multiplying these primes unveiled a website, marked by a countdown and a cicada symbol. As the countdown concluded, the site revealed a set of global coordinates with the directive, "Seek our emblem at the nearest location to you."

As Cicada 3301 released physical coordinates worldwide, the challenge transformed from a complex online enigma into a global real-life treasure hunt. Spanning five countries with 14 unique coordinates, the vast scale of this operation hinted to participants that Cicada 3301 might be more than just an elaborate digital diversion.

Pursuing these coordinates, seekers encountered flyers featuring a QR code alongside a cicada image. Scanning the QR code led to another cicada depiction, embedded with a riddle. This riddle was a gateway to a subsequent puzzle, ultimately guiding to a website. Unknown to the participants, this was a race against time.

The website, a culmination of the QR code and its related challenges, was on a countdown. Those who unraveled the QR code riddle swiftly were faced with two possibilities: either they gained access to the puzzle's final stage or they encountered a message underscoring the creators' preference for 'the best, not the followers.' Speed was essential; only the quickest were permitted to advance, with a stern warning to keep the following stages confidential.

After the select few presumably reached the conclusion or were defeated by the ultimate challenge, Cicada 3301 faded into silence, leaving no further clues or puzzles. This lull was broken a month later by an announcement on the same subreddit used previously, declaring the conclusion of the puzzles and the successful recruitment of the "highly intelligent individuals" they sought.

One year to the day after the enigmatic debut of the original Cicada 3301 puzzle, a fresh image surfaced on 4chan, reigniting the intrigue and fervor of the digital sleuthing community. In the interceding year, numerous imitations had emerged, attempting to capitalize on the mystique of the original puzzle. However, it was the distinct PGP signature of this new image that authenticated its lineage, unmistakably signifying the return of the original creators and the reactivation of their quest for intellectual acumen.

This second chapter of the Cicada 3301 saga retained the foundational structure of its predecessor, weaving a complex web of challenges that tested the mettle of participants. Yet, it introduced innovative dimensions to the puzzle. Notably, it incorporated puzzles that required deciphering audio files, adding a layer of auditory analysis that had not been present in the original. Furthermore, the integration of a Twitter account into the puzzle's framework marked a step towards more contemporary forms of digital communication, expanding the scope and interactivity of the challenge.

The culmination of the 2013 puzzles mirrored the previous year's climactic approach, involving a series of global coordinates. These coordinates, spanning diverse geographical locations, led intrepid solvers to find physical posters. Each poster, much like the previous year, was adorned with a QR code, serving as a gateway to the subsequent phase of the puzzle.

As participants across the globe engaged with this new set of challenges, they demonstrated remarkable skill and determination, dissecting each layer of the puzzle with keen insight and collaborative effort. Despite the collective intelligence and resourcefulness of the community, the final stages of the puzzle remained as enigmatic and elusive as the organization behind it.

Unlike the previous year, where the conclusion of the puzzle was marked by a post on a subreddit indicating the successful recruitment of "highly intelligent individuals," the 2013 iteration of Cicada 3301 concluded without such closure. The lack of a final, conclusive message left the ultimate fate of the puzzle and its solvers shrouded in mystery. This absence of closure only fueled further speculation and discussion within the online community, with many pondering the true intentions and identities of the puzzle's creators, as well as the fate of those who might have successfully navigated to the end of this cryptic and challenging journey.

A year after the second installment of the Cicada 3301 puzzles, the enigmatic group resurfaced with yet another challenging image. In a departure from their previous pattern, the 2014 puzzle made its first appearance on Twitter, now known as Platform X, diverging from the traditional 4chan platform. This shift in platform choice hinted at an evolution in the approach of Cicada 3301, possibly reflecting a broader reach or a change in strategy. As with the earlier puzzles, this initial image served as a portal into a deep and complex labyrinth of cryptic challenges, each more intricate than the last.

The 2014 series of puzzles introduced a significant and intriguing element that set it apart from the previous years: the Liber Primus, a book steeped in mystery and symbolism. This tome was a collection of pages filled with symbols, many of which had been subtly introduced in the puzzles of the preceding years. The Liber Primus not only linked the puzzles of 2014 to the legacy of Cicada 3301 but also presented a formidable challenge in itself. It was an amalgamation of cryptic writings and smaller, nested puzzles, all written in a symbolic language that demanded exceptional cryptographic skills to decipher.

The segments of the Liber Primus that were successfully decoded revealed a rich tapestry of ideological musings and philosophies, possibly hinting at the motivations and beliefs of the Cicada 3301 creators. Despite the concerted efforts of a dedicated community of solvers, a substantial portion of the Liber Primus remains undeciphered to this day, presenting an enduring enigma and a tantalizing beacon for cryptographers and puzzle enthusiasts around the world.

After the 2014 puzzles, the trail of Cicada 3301 went cold, with no new puzzles emerging. However, in 2016, a verifiable communication from Cicada 3301 broke the silence, cryptically stating that the "Liber Primus is the way," suggesting that the key to understanding Cicada 3301, or perhaps a yet-undiscovered puzzle, lay within its pages. This was followed by another rare post in 2017, a cautionary message warning of "false paths," which further mystified the community and fueled speculation about the true nature and purpose of these puzzles.

Since then, the silence from Cicada 3301 has been deafening, leaving the puzzle-solving community in a state of suspense and anticipation. The lack of new puzzles or updates has only deepened the mystery surrounding Cicada 3301, turning it into a legend in the annals of internet lore. The enigmatic nature of Cicada 3301, combined with the unfinished challenge of the Liber Primus, continues to captivate and challenge a global audience, eager for any sign or clue that might unravel the mysteries left by this most elusive of digital enigmas.

The enigmatic puzzles of Cicada 3301, shrouded in mystery and intrigue, commenced with cryptic images that beckoned the brightest minds into a labyrinth of riddles. These images were not mere visuals but gateways to a world of hidden clues, messages, and ciphers, each meticulously woven into their fabric. Among them, QR codes stood as puzzles within puzzles, offering keys to further enigmatic layers when deciphered. Other images utilized visual illusions and the subtle art of steganography, embedding secret texts within the very pixels of the image, challenging solvers to look beyond the apparent.

However, the challenges of Cicada 3301 transcended visual boundaries, venturing into the realm of auditory enigmas. Among these, the spectrogram puzzles were particularly fascinating, presenting audio tracks whose waveforms, when visually represented, concealed cryptic messages or codes. Participants were tasked with converting these auditory puzzles into visual formats, unraveling the hidden clues embedded within.

The journey through Cicada 3301's puzzles was also a journey through literature and history. Participants encountered references to classic literary works and historical texts, requiring not just recognition but a deep understanding of these references to progress further. This aspect of the challenge tested the solver's literary acumen and their ability to draw thematic connections, weaving a rich tapestry of culture and cryptography.

The cryptographic elements of Cicada 3301 were both diverse and complex. Participants grappled with a range of ciphers, from the simpler Caesar and Vigenère ciphers to more intricate and obscure algorithms. Deciphering these cryptic messages often unveiled the path to the subsequent phase, making cryptography skills crucial in the quest for solutions.

The puzzles often extended into the digital realm, leading participants to various websites and online platforms. Here, the challenge lay in dissecting and analyzing hidden information, which could involve delving into web page source codes, deciphering URL patterns, or uncovering links to concealed or secured content.

The quintessence of Cicada 3301's puzzles lay in their multi-layered complexity. Each solved puzzle was but a step in a longer, more intricate journey, with each layer unraveling only to reveal another, deeper mystery. This structure demanded not only intelligence and skill from the solvers but also unwavering perseverance and vigilance, as they navigated through the convoluted and captivating world of Cicada 3301's legendary puzzles.

Cicada 3301's enigmatic puzzles captivated a vast, international community of enthusiasts, drawn together by a shared zeal for intellectual pursuits and a collective curiosity to unravel the mysteries of this cryptic challenge. This eclectic group, hailing from various corners of the globe, found common ground in their online collaboration, pooling together their diverse expertise in cryptography, computer science, and numerous other fields. The phenomenon underscored the internet's remarkable ability to connect individuals from different backgrounds and cultures in the pursuit of solving intricate and complex problems.

The allure and intrigue of Cicada 3301's puzzles have led to numerous individuals across the internet claiming to have progressed to the advanced stages of the puzzle series. However, verifying these claims is a challenging endeavor, with only a handful of these assertions being credibly substantiated.

Among the noteworthy individuals who have engaged with these puzzles is Joel Eriksson, who notably advanced to the QR code phase. His journey, however, met an abrupt end with a message indicating his pace hadn't matched the required speed. Another solver, Marcus Wanner, progressed even further. He shared insights into the subsequent phase, which involved probing questions about beliefs on privacy and freedom. Wanner described encountering a secretive website intended for communication among the finalists, where they were assigned tasks. Regrettably, his journey too came to an unexpected halt as he failed to complete these tasks swiftly, leading to the abrupt closure of the website. These narratives from Eriksson and Wanner add layers of intrigue and complexity to the already enigmatic puzzle of Cicada 3301, painting a picture of a challenge that is as elusive as it is captivating.

The enigma of Cicada 3301, with its puzzling cessation, has left a trail of unanswered questions and profound mysteries in its wake. The identities and motives of the people or entity orchestrating this elaborate endeavor remain shrouded in secrecy, fueling widespread speculation and intrigue. The core of the mystery lies in the recruitment process — was it ever completed by anyone, and if so, to what end? This phenomenon stands as a powerful symbol of the undying fascination with unsolved riddles and cryptic challenges that continues to captivate the digital world.

Narratives from individuals like Marcus Wanner, who attempted to solve these puzzles, hint at the existence of a secretive organization driven by a commitment to ideals of freedom and privacy. Yet, the specifics of these ideals and the organization's overarching objectives remain elusive, obscured by the scant information that has surfaced. This paucity of concrete details has ignited a frenzy of speculation, leading many to ponder the possible identities of the creators and the ultimate purpose of these enigmatic puzzles.

With its creators' identities and intentions cloaked in secrecy, a multitude of theories and conjectures have arisen. These range from it being a sophisticated tool for government recruitment to a mere elaborate art project, or even an intricate prank. The absence of solid information about the minds behind this phenomenon only amplifies the allure and mystery surrounding it.

One widely discussed theory posits that Cicada 3301 is a sophisticated recruitment mechanism employed by a government agency or an intelligence outfit. Supporters of this idea point to the puzzles' complexity, the intellectual acumen required to solve them, and the nature of the challenges as indicative of a screening process for potential intelligence operatives. Some even suggest that those who crack the code are discreetly absorbed into secret government missions.

Alternatively, there's a belief that Cicada 3301 might be an induction method for a secret society or even a cult. The elaborate nature of the puzzles and the aura of exclusivity that envelopes the challenges have led to speculations about it being a gateway to an elite, covert organization. This line of thought often intertwines with the mythology of groups like the Illuminati, believed by some to be puppeteers of global events.

In the realm of digital expertise, some conspiracy theorists argue that Cicada 3301 is a front for groups specializing in hacking or cybersecurity. They theorize that the challenges are a means to scout and recruit talented hackers and cybersecurity professionals for various undisclosed activities, potentially including cyber espionage.

Conversely, a more benign interpretation is that Cicada 3301 is an extensive art project or a social experiment. Proponents of this view argue that the primary purpose of the puzzles is to stimulate intellectual curiosity and creativity, with the elements of secrecy and exclusivity adding to the overall experimental nature of the project.

The saga of Cicada 3301 stands as one of the internet's most captivating mysteries, transcending its origins in online forums to become a source of fascination and intrigue for a broad audience. This enigmatic puzzle has sparked a widespread quest for understanding, captivating those who delve into its secrets. Regardless of whether it's perceived as a recruitment challenge, a complex art project, or an intricate game.

In 2021, the intrigue around Cicada 3301 took a cinematic turn with the release of "Dark Web: Cicada 3301." Directed by and featuring Alan Ritchson, known for his lead role in Prime Video's "Reacher," this film offers a fictionalized and more ominous interpretation of the Cicada 3301 phenomenon.

Despite the absence of new Cicada 3301 challenges, its legacy endures through vibrant online puzzle-solving communities, the ignited intellectual curiosity, and the sustained interest in cryptographic challenges. It epitomizes the internet's enigmatic side, highlighting the allure of anonymity and the significant influence of online communities in generating captivating phenomena.

Lostwave

Lostwave represents a fascinating digital era phenomenon, emerging as a unique internet term that encapsulates the mystery and allure surrounding music and songs that exist without any traceable information about their artist, title, or origins. This enigmatic term was birthed on the bustling forums of Reddit in 2019, amid the fervent online quest to unveil the identity of a piece known as "The Most Mysterious Song on the Internet." This quest rapidly expanded, leading to the creation of a dedicated subreddit where enthusiasts and digital detectives alike converged to unravel the mysteries of other unknown songs, such as the intriguing "Everyone Knows That (Ulterior Motives)."

The allure of Lostwave primarily stems from its roots in the pre-internet age, with a significant portion of these auditory enigmas hailing from the vibrant and experimental eras of the 1980s and 1990s. However, the Lostwave phenomenon isn't confined to these decades alone; it spans across various periods in history, weaving a tapestry of forgotten melodies and elusive tunes from different times.

Intriguingly, the term "Lostwave" is a creative portmanteau, ingeniously blending the word "lost" with "wave," linking it conceptually to other well-known music genres such as "new wave," "cold wave," and "vaporwave." This nomenclature reflects not only the lost status of these musical pieces but also their undulating presence in the vast ocean of internet music culture, where they ride the waves of digital rediscovery and collective curiosity.

This term, therefore, becomes a beacon for music aficionados and cultural archaeologists, guiding them through the foggy waters of forgotten melodies in their quest to uncover and reclaim lost pieces of musical history.

The Most Mysterious Song on the Internet

In the shadows of the Cold War era, a tale of musical mystery unfolded, woven by a man named Darius S. His role in this enigmatic narrative began in the vibrant cultural landscape of West Germany, where he found himself enchanted by the eclectic sounds emanating from Norddeutscher Rundfunk, a prominent public radio station. It was here, amidst the airwaves carrying the soulful tunes of the 1980s, that Darius stumbled upon a song—a melody that would soon weave its way into the fabric of internet folklore.

Armed with a cassette tape and a keen ear for music, Darius embarked on a meticulous endeavor to capture the essence of this era. His tape became a treasure trove of auditory gems, featuring not just the mysterious song but also tracks from iconic bands like XTC and The Cure. In his quest for sonic perfection, Darius skillfully excised the radio hosts' dialogues, a decision that, while ensuring crisp recordings, inadvertently shrouded the mysterious song's origins in deeper mystery, erasing its airplay date and title from history.

As the years rolled on, 1985 marked a pivotal moment in this auditory odyssey. Darius, perhaps driven by a mix of nostalgia and curiosity, curated a playlist of these unidentified songs, a testament to his enduring fascination with these lost melodies. Fast forward to 2004, and the narrative takes a digital turn. Lydia H., Darius's older sister, gifted him a doorway to the digital world—a website domain for his birthday. Seizing this opportunity, Darius ventured into the realm of digital archiving, meticulously converting his cherished playlist into .aiff and .m4a files. The website domain became his beacon, illuminating the existence of this playlist to the world, a siren call to fellow music detectives and enthusiasts.

The quest for the song's identity reached a crescendo on March 18, 2007. Lydia, under the intriguing pseudonym "Anton Riedel," took to the digital landscape, her determination unyielding. She initially cast her queries into the depths of Usenet, specifically the group de.rec.musik.recherche, a haven for music inquiries. But her search didn't stop there; it expanded, reaching out to the corners of the internet where music communities thrived. She posted excerpts of this enigmatic song on best-of-80s.de, a German forum that celebrated the synth-pop era of the eighties, and on spiritofradio.ca, a tribute site to the Canadian radio station CFNY-FM, known for its eclectic playlists.

This digital expedition, spearheaded by Lydia and anchored by Darius's early recordings, transformed into a collective quest, engaging a global community of netizens, each driven by a shared desire to unravel the mystery of this lost song. Their journey, spanning decades and crossing the digital divide, stands as a testament to the enduring power of music and the unyielding curiosity of the human spirit in the quest to reclaim a piece of forgotten history.

In 2019, the enigmatic journey to uncover the origins of an unidentified song transformed into a viral sensation, igniting the curiosity of a global online community. At the heart of this digital-age detective story was Gabriel da Silva Vieira, a Brazilian teenager. His quest began when Nicolás Zúñiga of the Spanish indie record label Dead Wax Records introduced him to this auditory mystery. Fueled by a blend of curiosity and determination, Gabriel took to YouTube and numerous music-centric Reddit communities, sharing an excerpt of the song. His efforts culminated in the creation of r/TheMysteriousSong, a subreddit dedicated to unearthing the song's elusive origins.

The story caught the attention of the Australian music news website Tone Deaf on May 27, 2019. Tyler Jenke, the author, delved into the initial stages of this intriguing search, drawing parallels to a similar quest in 2013 that successfully identified "On the Roof" by Swedish musician Johan Lindell. This article marked a significant milestone in the song's journey from an obscure melody to a subject of widespread fascination.

The narrative took another leap forward on July 9, 2019, when American YouTuber Justin Whang featured the song in an episode of his series "Tales from the Internet." His video, detailing the progress of the search, acted as a catalyst, mobilizing an even larger segment of the internet community to join in this collaborative quest.

In a remarkable twist, Reddit user u/johnnymetoo revealed the complete version of the song. This crucial piece of the puzzle was uncovered from a link in one of Lydia's Usenet posts before it was deleted, adding a new layer of depth to the ongoing investigation.

The search efforts expanded to include reaching out to potentially key figures, such as Paul Baskerville, a disc jockey from NDR, and GEMA, a German per-formance rights organization. Even a YouTube channel named "8ozforever," known for posting obscure music, was contacted in the hopes of shedding light on the song. On July 21, 2019, Baskerville showcased the song on his radio show Nachtclub, reigniting interest and awareness about the search. Although this didn't yield new leads, it played a crucial role in informing Lydia and Darius about the renewed efforts to solve the mystery.

In a turn of events, Lydia, familiar with the song from its early days, joined the Reddit community in August 2019. Her involvement bridged the gap between the song's mysterious past and its digital-age resurgence, bringing new perspectives and insights to an investigation that had captured the imagination of a global audience, all united in their quest to solve one of the internet's most captivating musical mysteries.

On a pivotal day, July 9, 2020, the Reddit community experienced a significant development in the ongoing quest to uncover the origins of the unidentified song. User u/FlexxonMobil, in a remarkable display of digital detective work, managed to acquire the complete list of songs played by Paul Baskerville on his

1984 show, Musik Für Junge Leute, and shared this treasure trove on Reddit. This discovery sparked a flurry of activity among users, who dove into the list with the hope of finally pinpointing the elusive song. However, after meticulous scrutiny, they reached a consensus: the song was nowhere to be found on that list, effectively debunking the theory that Baskerville was the original broadcaster.

The search continued undeterred, and by December 2020, the remaining Musik Für Junge Leute playlists had been obtained. The community embarked on an exhaustive examination of these lists, only to conclude, once again, that the mysterious song had not graced the airwaves of Musik Für Junge Leute.

In January 2021, another piece of the puzzle emerged. The community received playlists from other Baskerville shows, Der Club and Nachtclub, specifically from October and November 1984. Intriguingly, these playlists contained several songs that Darius and Lydia had recorded, including tracks from the BASF 4|1 tape. This discovery ignited a spark of hope within the community, leading them to believe that the unidentified song might be hidden within the remaining playlists.

Meanwhile, in late 2020, a Discord user named Fliere made a technical breakthrough. Analyzing the tape recording of the mysterious song, Fliere identified a distinct 10 kHz line, a signature also found in other songs from the BASF 4|1 and some from BASF 4|2. This subtle yet crucial detail revealed that this 10 kHz line was a characteristic of almost all NDR radio broadcasts at the time, but notably absent in broadcasts from Hilversum radio. This finding significantly narrowed down the possibilities, suggesting that the song was likely broadcasted on an NDR station.

The saga took another intriguing turn on November 2, 2021. Lydia shared a serendipitous discovery on Reddit: during the renovation of her apartment, one of her sons unearthed a box filled with old tapes, among which lay a higher quality version of the enigmatic song. Although the tracklist of this newly found tape differed from earlier ones, there was speculation that it might have been made from the same original recording, as it shared some of the same audio artifacts as the first tape.

This journey, marked by community collaboration, technological sleuthing, and unexpected discoveries, continued to captivate and engage a global audience, each step bringing them closer to unraveling the mystery of a song that had, for so long, eluded identification.

The quest to identify the mysterious song has seen a multitude of theories and speculations from searchers around the world. A general consensus among the searchers is that the singer likely has a European accent, although pinpointing the exact nature of the accent remains a challenge.

Among the various theories, one intriguing speculation revolves around the use of a Yamaha DX7 synthesizer in the song. This iconic instrument, which hit the market in late 1983, is thought by some users to be responsible for the distinctive leads heard in the track.

The timeline of the song's recording has been a subject of debate, with many speculating that it was recorded in 1984. This theory is bolstered by the fact that most of the other songs on Darius S.'s cassette tape hail from around the same period. Additionally, the type of Technics tape deck that Darius likely used to record the song was manufactured in 1984, lending further weight to this hypothesis.

Paul Baskerville, a key figure in the narrative, has stated that he does not recall playing the song. He hypothesizes that it might have been a demo recording, played once by an NDR presenter and subsequently discarded.

The most promising lead to date emerged from the research of Armin Linder, who published his findings in March 2021. After conducting numerous interviews, Linder suggested that the song was the creation of Viennese musicians Christian Brandl and Ronnie Urini. According to his research, they wrote the song in both German and English versions in 1983. The recording is believed to have taken place in the studio of the late Fred Jakesch on Mariahilferstraße in Vienna, with Brandl on vocals and Urini on drums. Although Heinz Hochrainer was present for a planned saxophone part, this element was never recorded. A preliminary mix of the song reportedly made its way to NRD Radio in 1984. Roni Urini corroborated this story and provided a typewritten version of the German lyrics as evidence, with Hochrainer also confirming the account.

However, doubts linger, mainly fueled by Robert Wolf, a close musical associate of Christian Brandl and the frontman of their joint band, Chuzpe. Wolf has expressed skepticism, noting that he does not recognize Brandl's voice in the song and suggesting that the drum sounds are more reminiscent of a Linn Drum machine than Urini's playing, a machine known to be used in Jakesch's studio. This lingering uncertainty keeps the mystery alive, as definitive proof remains elusive, and the search for the true origins of the song continues.

Everyone Knows That (Ulterior Motives)

"Everyone Knows That" (EKT), also known by intriguing aliases like "Ulterior Motives," "Shapes," and "Tell Me The Truth," is a fascinating enigma in the world of lost music. This mysterious song burst onto the digital scene in 2021, captivating the curiosity of music enthusiasts worldwide. Its story began with a brief, 17-second audio clip, exuding the charm of an old treasure. The clip, though low in quality, was enough to spark a widespread hunt for its origins.

The journey of EKT's snippet is as intriguing as its elusive nature. Uploaded on WatZatSong, a platform reminiscent of the early days of Shazam, the snippet was shared by a user known as carl92. This individual stumbled upon the clip in an old DVD backup, a discovery wrapped in layers of mystery and nostalgia.

Lacking any clue about its origins, carl92 turned to the vast expanse of the internet, hoping for answers.

The song's style, echoing the synth-pop vibrations of the 1980s and 1990s, led theorists to speculate about its time of creation. Rolling Stone even chimed in, likening its sound to the new wave music that defined the 80s. The snippet, intriguingly, bore a file date from 1999, suggesting a potential Spanish origin, as speculated by carl92, who was presumably based in Spain.

As 2022 and 2023 unfolded, "Everyone Knows That" found itself riding a new wave of popularity. The song's enigmatic allure led to the creation of a dedicated subreddit in June 2023, uniting music detectives and enthusiasts in a communal quest. This subreddit became a melting pot of theories, discussions, and continuous searches, reflecting the human penchant for solving mysteries and connecting over shared curiosities.

In essence, EKT is not just a lost song but a symbol of the timeless bond between music and memory, an embodiment of the collective yearning to uncover the hidden gems of our past.

The journey of uncovering the origins of the enigmatic song snippet, initially uploaded with little fanfare, gradually morphed into an enthralling quest with a cult-like following. This mysterious musical piece, after months of meticulous research and the elimination of numerous artists, sparked a widespread intrigue that extended its roots into the realms of Reddit. A dedicated subreddit emerged, becoming a hub for fervent discussions and theories about the song's elusive origins.

The speculations about the source of this snippet were as diverse as they were imaginative. Theories ranged from it being a relic of a 1990s MTV broadcast, a catchy commercial jingle, to a piece of Japanese Musak that once floated through the air of McDonald's across Eastern Europe. Despite the widespread speculation, one distributor of muzak confirmed the absence of this track in their records, deepening the mystery.

Adding to the intrigue, several YouTube users, fueled by curiosity and creativity, ventured to expand this tantalizing snippet into full-length songs. These covers, including those generated by AI, painted YouTube with a palette of imaginative interpretations of the elusive track.

The quest for the song's creator opened a Pandora's box of possibilities. Names like the Swedish band Roxette and the Australian duo Savage Garden floated in the sea of speculation. Some even toyed with the idea that the snippet was a product of artificial intelligence, though this theory met with skepticism from many.

Roxette, known for their distinctive sound, became a prime suspect due to perceived similarities in the snippet. Some users, after altering the pitch of the clip, reported hearing a female vocalist, reminiscent of the style employed by Roxette in hits like "Dangerous." Moreover, the bass tones in the snippet drew parallels with Guy Pratt, a renowned session bassist from the 1980s. Yet, despite these correlations, doubts lingered, primarily due to Roxette's distinct and recognizable style.

Savage Garden, catapulted to fame with their 1997 debut album, also emerged as potential creators. The snippet's vocals bore a resemblance to Darren Hayes, Savage Garden's lead vocalist. This theory gained momentum on November 17, 2023, when Hayes cryptically posted "Everyone Knows That" on the social media platform X, sending ripples of speculation and renewed interest across the internet.

Ready 'n' Steady

"Ready 'n' Steady," a song shrouded in mystery and intrigue for decades, is a remarkable tale in the annals of music history. Crafted by the American duo Dennis Lucchesi and Jim Franks, this enigmatic track found its way onto the Billboard magazine's Bubbling Under the Hot 100 chart in June 1979. Intriguingly, the artist was credited as D. A., a moniker derived from Lucchesi's first and middle initials, a name he had adopted during his days as a regional performer.

For years, the true identity behind "D.A." and the song itself vanished into the annals of music history. No recordings of "Ready 'n' Steady" could be found, no physical evidence of its existence surfaced, turning it into a "phantom record" in the eyes of collectors and music aficionados. This lack of evidence led many to speculate whether the song ever existed at all, fueling a mystique that surrounded it for decades.

The saga of "Ready 'n' Steady" took a dramatic turn in 2016, thanks to the dogged determination of researcher Paul Haney. Diving deep into copyright records, Haney unraveled the threads of this long-standing mystery, finally bringing to light the elusive recording, offering the public its first-ever glimpse into this musical enigma.

The journey of "Ready 'n' Steady" in the Billboard charts is a tale in itself. Featured in the June 16, 1979 issue, the song was among the ten records on the Bubbling Under Hot 100 Singles chart. This special chart was known for showcasing songs that were on the cusp of breaking into Billboard's prestigious Hot 100, starting from position number 101. "Ready 'n' Steady" debuted at the number 106 spot, making a modest yet significant presence among its peers.

The record, released under the Rascal label, showed a promising ascent in the following weeks. It climbed to the 103rd position on June 23, and further inched up to number 102 the next week. However, this upward trajectory was short-lived as the song soon disappeared from the charts. This brief appearance and subsequent vanishing act only added to the song's allure and the mystery surrounding its existence.

The story of "Ready 'n' Steady" is not just about a song; it's a narrative that encapsulates the mystique of lost art, the relentless pursuit of music historians, and the joy of uncovering hidden gems from the past. It's a testament to the enduring power of music and the intrigue that can persist for decades, capturing the imagination of generations of music lovers.

Joel Whitburn, a renowned music historian and the driving force behind Record Research Inc., has dedicated his career to the meticulous study of the Billboard charts. His company's expertise is showcased through various publications containing extensive chart data. Over the years, Whitburn amassed an impressive collection of records, encompassing every 45 rpm single that ever graced the Hot 100 or Bubbling Under charts, with one notable exception: the elusive "Ready 'n' Steady."

In a 1995 interview, Whitburn revealed a fascinating detail about his quest for this phantom record. Despite his extensive research and vast collection, he admitted to never having seen or heard "Ready 'n' Steady." However, he shared intriguing speculations about the record's origins. Whitburn hypothesized that it might have been the work of a female punk rock group from Chicago, dating back to 1979. Further adding to the mystery, he suggested that the Rascal label, under which the record was supposedly released, originated from a residential address in Detroit.

Whitburn's investigative efforts led him to a punk rock publication, which contained a small advertisement for the Rascal label in Detroit. Acting on this lead, he had the address checked, only to discover a desolate and boarded-up house, deepening the enigma surrounding the record. Notably, "Ready 'n' Steady" was cataloged as number 102 under the Rascal label, leaving the existence of a Rascal 101, if any, unknown to collectors.

In the 2005 fourth edition of Whitburn's "Bubbling Under the Hot 100" book, a significant amendment was made to the entry for "D. A." A note was added, casting doubt on the very existence of the record and artist, and it was valued at $150. However, by 2009, when Whitburn released his latest "Top Pop Singles" book, which included both Hot 100 and Bubbling Under singles, the mysterious D. A. was conspicuously absent. In a conversation with CelebrityAccess, Whitburn expressed his skepticism about the existence of "Ready 'n' Steady," even pondering if its chart listing was a deliberate copyright trap set by Billboard.

Adding another layer to the story, the 2002 16th edition of Jerry Osborne's "Official Price Guide to Records" also listed "Ready 'n' Steady," assigning it a value of $75–$125. Intriguingly, the guide mentioned an unnamed LP on the Frontline label, dated around 1985 or 1986. This record was identified as "Fearful Symmetry" by the Christian rock band Daniel Amos, which occasionally used the abbreviation "D.A." This discovery further complicated the quest to unravel the mystery of "Ready 'n' Steady," leaving collectors and historians alike pondering the true story behind this phantom record.

The intriguing saga of "Ready & Steady" is deeply intertwined with the annals of the United States Copyright Office. In this repository of creative works, there exists a registration for a song titled "Ready & Steady," attributed to the creative partnership of D. A. Lucchesi and Jim Franks. This record, filed on September 16, 1986, acknowledges a creation date going back to 1979. Dennis Armand "D. A." Lucchesi, born on June 5, 1945, and passing away on August 18, 2005, was more than just a name in a registry. He was a Californian mortgage broker with a passion for music, performing part-time under the moniker "D. A. and the Dukes."

The mystery of "Ready & Steady" took a significant turn in 2016, thanks to the tenacity and curiosity of Paul Haney from Record Research Inc. Haney's investigation into the song's copyright registration led him to Jim Franks, one of the song's co-authors. In a groundbreaking development, Franks provided Haney with a recording of the elusive song. Haney revealed that the song had been recorded by the producer Steve Cropper, yet it never saw the light of day as a vinyl record, nor was it ever available for sale.

The circumstances surrounding the song's appearance on the Billboard charts are as mysterious as the song itself. According to Haney, a record promoter with connections to a major label took an interest in the band and managed to place the song on the Billboard chart. This extraordinary feat made "Ready 'n' Steady" a unique entity in music history – it became the only song to ever appear on any Billboard chart without having been commercially released. The Rascal label, which was tied to the song, existed merely as a concept on paper at the time and was owned by a relative of one of the band members. It wasn't until 1984 that Rascal, based in Hollywood, would release a few independent singles, but none were attributed to D.A.

The public debut of "Ready 'n' Steady" on the airwaves occurred in an unexpected venue. It was on July 8, 2016, during an episode of the "Crap from the Past" radio show broadcasted on KFAI in Minneapolis, Minnesota. On this show, hosted by music aficionados, the recording of "Ready 'n' Steady" was finally played on the radio, marking the first time the song was heard by a broader audience. This momentous airing not only ended decades of speculation and mystery but also solidified the song's place in the fascinating tapestry of music history.

Your Eyes (Come Back 2 Me)

The mysterious journey of the song "Your Eyes" on the internet is a fascinating tale that spans years and crosses continents. It first emerged in 2003 on a Chinese website, nestled within a compilation known as   359 (New Song Hot Dance Album 359), curated by an enigmatic DJ whose identity remains unknown as of February 2021. This compilation, a melting pot of various tracks, included "Your Eyes," intriguingly labeled as Pop (European and American lyrical high-end pop), leaving the song nameless and adding to its mystique. Alongside "Your Eyes," the compilation featured other obscure songs, some of which have become lost over time, further deepening the mystery.

As 2003 gave way to 2004, the compilation, along with "Your Eyes," began to ripple across other Chinese websites, gaining modest traction on platforms like 666c.com and real2000.org. In October 2004, the song found a new digital home on hcdj.com, still carrying the same enigmatic file name from its original compilation. Its journey didn't stop there; it eventually made its way to another popular Chinese site, QQMusic.com.

The song's odyssey took another turn sometime between 2003 and 2009. During this period, a user named DaRioXYK stumbled upon "Your Eyes" on an unspecified website. The version he found was of low quality, with the intro regrettably cut off. Undeterred, DaRioXYK brought the song to a broader audience by uploading it to YouTube in December 2009 under the title Italodance Sconosciuta/Unknown Italodance. Whether he discovered it on one of the aforementioned Chinese websites remains a tantalizing unknown. For a long while, this YouTube snippet, flawed yet captivating, was the only glimpse of "Your Eyes" available to the world, until a significant development occurred in 2020, rekindling interest in this elusive musical piece.

The enigmatic journey of the song "Your Eyes" between 2009 and 2020 was marked by a series of intriguing but ultimately misleading leads. The first of these came from an individual who asserted that the song was "Radio Rise" by Mistic Moment. However, this claim was soon debunked as a hoax; the individual had merely created a fake edit of the snippet originally posted by DaRioXYK.

Later, a user on Discogs stirred the pot by claiming the song's title was "Your

Eyes (Come Back 2 Me)" by Gabry-L. Despite not being conclusively disproved, multiple indicators suggested that this, too, was a fabrication. Adding to the confusion, the same edit previously attributed to Mistic Moment resurfaced in December 2019 under the name Gabry-L - Your Eyes (Come Back 2 Me), further muddling the song's true identity.

Another lead emerged in 2018, involving a remix of "Your Eyes" by DJ JPedroza, who credited an unknown artist named MCW. Initially, there was speculation that MCW might be the original artist of "Your Eyes." However, it was later revealed that MCW was actually a pseudonym for Michael Waust, who was not the song's original artist but had collaborated with DJ JPedroza on the remix.

Finally, there was speculation that the mysterious Italodance track was "Jungle Eyes" by The Test ft Rodger. This theory was put to rest in January 2021 when the song was located and found not to match the elusive "Your Eyes."

On a significant day in the history of the song "Your Eyes," April 4, 2020, the internet saw two key developments. First, a YouTube user named johnson paul uploaded a complete low-quality version of "Your Eyes," which included the intro missing from the snippet shared by DaRioXYK. This version was sourced from QQMusic. On the same day, another YouTube user, Aigeng, shared just the intro in high quality, but it was part of a remix featured in a radio broadcast. Initially, Aigeng mentioned restrictions related to copyright as a reason for not sharing the title, but it later became apparent that even he was uncertain of the song's true name.

During this period, there was speculation that "Your Eyes" might be "Angel Eyes" by Che JT, a track confirmed to exist by its label, DIY Records. However, no recording of this track has been found as of February 2021. Further investigation suggested that Che JT might be an abbreviation for Che JianTao, who, upon contact, had no knowledge of "Your Eyes."

In May 2020, the mystery deepened when a YouTuber named Mike B uploaded a high-quality radio edit of "Your Eyes." It was later revealed that he had created this edit himself using a full high-quality version of the song. The title of the track remained unknown to him as well, despite the growing demand for information.

The early months of 2021 brought another twist. The original Chinese compilation featuring "Your Eyes" was finally uncovered, confirming its widespread distribution across various Chinese websites. Additionally, in February 2021, an intriguing entry titled "I Need You" was found in the GEMA database. The artists associated with this entry were known Italodance artists, and the label involved was also responsible for Che JT's "Angel Eyes." This discovery added another layer to the ongoing puzzle surrounding the true identity of "Your Eyes."

Poor Christmas

In the enigmatic world of lost music, a song titled "Poor-Christmas," also known by its intriguing alternate titles "Eyes of Love" and "Come On," stands out as a particularly mysterious piece. This song, recorded in the autumnal ambiance of October 1987 in Germany, carries with it a story that intertwines the realms of music, mystery, and digital archaeology.

The artist behind "Poor-Christmas" is an individual known as René, who also goes by the intriguing moniker DeDiniDevil. René's contribution to the world of obscure music is not limited to this song alone; he is also recognized for recording another enigmatic track titled "On The Roof."

The origins of "Poor-Christmas" trace back to its recording from an un-specified German radio station. The exact station remains unknown, but speculations include names such as Radio FFN, Hessen 3, or NDR 2, the latter being particularly noted for its association with "The Most Mysterious Song on the Internet." The original recording was made on a nondescript cassette by René M., and it's believed that the song's title and artist might have been announced during the broadcast. René recalls the song being titled either "Poor Christmas" or "Your Christmas" and performed by a band possibly named "The Face."

The tale takes another turn with René's creation of a website named De-DiniDevil, sometime before 2004. This site featured a section dedicated to "wanted" mysterious songs, becoming a beacon for those intrigued by musical enigmas. Although the exact date when "Poor-Christmas" was first featured on the site is uncertain, it's speculated to have been around 2001. The site gained a degree of notoriety within certain communities, particularly because of another song it featured, known at the time as "Stay (The Second Time Around)," which garnered considerable appreciation.

The saga began a new chapter on September 16, 2007, when an individual named René R. shared the song on spiritofradio.ca. His quest to identify the song had already spanned over three years, yet his post initially went unnoticed.

Fast forward to September 2013, the song "Stay (The Second Time Around)" sparked a viral sensation and was swiftly identified, casting a renewed spotlight on the DeDiniDevil website where "Poor-Christmas" was also listed. In an effort to broaden its reach, René R., under the username Osterhase8, uploaded the song to YouTube on March 31, 2015.

The intrigue surrounding "Poor-Christmas" surged in 2020, especially within The Mysterious Song Discord server, where enthusiasts dedicated a special channel to its investigation. In October of that year, new insights emerged, including René's recollections of the recording session and a list of potential radio stations from which the song could have originated.

The Discord community pursued various leads. They explored songs such as

"Christmas Day" by The Reflection, "Dance Away (Christmas Day)" by The Present, and "Steal Her Away (This Christmas)" by Face 2 Face. By February 2021, the first two bands were eliminated from consideration, with Face 2 Face remaining a plausible candidate, especially since René remembered the band's name as "The Face."

On November 25, 2021, Rene M. (the original poster) uploaded a full-length, redigitized version of the recording to his YouTube channel, MellieTerry, providing a clearer version for further analysis.

The plot thickened on July 3, 2022, when a Discord user named Isle7 shared the audio of "Steal Her Away (This Christmas)," confirming that it was not the sought-after song.

In a recent development in September 2023, a Reddit user named East-Yam-1602 proposed that the song could be "Face Of Grace – Why / Hear Me," a lead originating from a comment on the full version's YouTube upload. This suggestion sparked new interest, and efforts were made to contact a seller on Discogs to verify this lead. The search for the true identity of "Poor-Christmas" continues, fueled by a community of music detectives united by their shared fascination with this elusive song.

Lostwave August 2019

In August 2019, the r/lostwave subreddit witnessed a captivating post from u/IntelligentBread5, featuring a profoundly distorted song that quickly garnered intrigue. Dubbed "Lostwave August 2019", this song's moniker reflects its discovery time and location. The backstory is as intriguing as the audio itself: during a European journey, possibly in Northern England, the poster stumbled upon a treasure trove of cassette tapes at a yard sale, including works from iconic artists like Nirvana, AC/DC, and Michael Jackson. Among these, a sun-bleached tape marked only with the number "4" stood out.

This tape, despite its weathered condition, contained a track that piqued the poster's curiosity – LWA19. Amidst speculation, the audio's severe distortion, originally attributed to tape damage, sparked debates with many suggesting digital tampering in a software like Audacity. Adding to the mystery, only a 30-second snippet, known as "nah_nah_nah.mp3", remains of the original post, leaving the rest to the realms of speculation and enigma.

Shortly after the initial reveal, the original poster (OP) returned with a captivating update – a "remastered" version of the enigmatic tape. This new digital rendition, enhanced by a friend's expert pitch management, became the definitive version of LWA19, as the original audio was largely lost.

Intrigue around LWA19 surged, thanks to two key features by YouTuber cwschultz in September 2019 and March 2020, as part of his 'Mysterious Music' series. These deep dives into the song's mysteries reignited public interest by the summer of 2020, leading to a flurry of requests directed at u/IntelligentBread5. Fans were eager for a glimpse of the cassette and the remaining tracks, which the OP claimed were by the same band but in poorer quality than LWA19. He expressed intentions to release these after a friend's digitalization, but then, in a twist, deleted his Reddit account.

This deletion sparked a frenzied search, but progress was hampered by a troll masquerading as u/IntelligentBread5. This imposter released what they claimed was "the rest of the tape", but the content – church songs starkly different in style and quality from LWA19 – was quickly identified as fraudulent. One notable faux pas by the troll was the conspicuous sound of chip eating while recording, a clumsy attempt to mimic the original distortions of LWA19.

The saga of LWA19 took a turn when a troll's attempt to derail the search with a fake tape raised doubts about the original story itself. The community began to speculate whether the distortions in LWA19 were truly due to tape damage or the result of digital manipulation, possibly using software like Audacity. This suspicion intensified following u/IntelligentBread5's abrupt and convenient disappearance, just as demands for proof of the cassette and additional songs escalated.

Further investigations led to a consensus that the distortions were indeed digitally created. As a result, The Mysterious Song Discord server, once a hub for investigation, decided to discontinue their dedicated search channel, deeming the pursuit no longer worthwhile. Yet, there remained a belief that beneath the digital alterations, a genuine song existed, one that was not a creation of u/IntelligentBread5. The challenge, however, lay in the distorted lyrics, which made identifying the song's title or artist nearly impossible.

In the face of these daunting odds, The Lost Search Discord server continues its quest. One approach involves extensive remastering efforts by user antonio113#0576, aiming to clarify as many lyrics as possible. However, interpretations of the lyrics vary widely among users, suggesting that simple remastering may not yield clear results.

The server has also embarked on an ambitious project to recreate the song. While the lyrics of LWA19 are muddled, its structure and instrumental elements are discernible, offering a foundation for reconstruction. The goal is to produce a high-quality cover that could be more easily recognized by someone familiar with the original song. In this endeavor, YouTuber DefyJoe, known for covering other mysterious songs, has stepped up to the challenge, hoping that a clearer version might reach someone who can identify the original track. As of February 2021, this project is underway, offering a glimmer of hope in unraveling the enigma of LWA19.

Stay By My Side

"Stay By My Side," alternatively known as "Dream Your Dream" or "Dusk Tonight," is a captivating and enigmatic song, believed to have its roots in Greek discotheques. The journey of this mysterious melody through the digital world began on March 5, 2008, when a user known as Jugge introduced a 49-second snippet of SBMS on spiritofradio.ca, intriguingly leaving out any background story and the intro of the song.

The plot thickened later that year, on December 22, when a man named Konstantinos brought the same tune to the limelight on WatZatSong. This time, it was the full version, shared via zshare, a platform that has since vanished into the annals of internet history. Konstantinos intriguingly remarked that the song's tempo was excessively fast.

Fast forward to March 2009, a user going by the moniker 'DJK' emerged on the scene, fervently seeking to unravel the mystery of several songs, SBMS included. His posts, referencing the same SBMS link shared by Konstantinos on WZS, sparked renewed interest. In a twist of events, DJK mentioned an attempt to discuss the song on New Wave Outpost, but as of February 2021, this intriguing post remains an elusive piece of the puzzle.

In June 2009, a captivating twist unfolded on a forum post, where Konstantinos, a figure central to the mystery of the song "Stay By My Side," revealed a crucial detail. He indicated that this enigmatic tune originated from an old Greek disco compilation tape, suggesting its European essence.

Fast forward to August 2020, a significant development occurred. The snippets previously posted by Konstantinos on WatZatSong and Jugge on spiritofradio.ca were ingeniously merged into an extended version by a user named BSP015, breathing new life into the search.

In October of the same year, Jugge, another key player in this musical saga, was reached out to. He recalled receiving the song from an unknown source, fueling speculation that this mystery individual might be Konstantinos himself.

March 1, 2021, marked a pivotal moment. Following the resolution of another song mystery titled "Calling," Konstantinos, who had been absent from the scene for years, reemerged to express gratitude towards the community's relentless search efforts. Seizing this moment of renewed activity, a user named nonoseacrest broached the subject of SBMS. Responding promptly the next day, Konstantinos uploaded the full version of the song to WeTransfer. Accompanying this revelation, Konstantinos shared his past hobby of collecting cassettes from flea markets between 1994 and 2004, expressing his fondness for mid-80s synth pop, minimal, and Euro disco genres, often sourced from discotheques and pirate radio stations.

Despite these developments, the song's origins remain shrouded in mystery. One Reddit user notably pondered over the similarity of the voice to Phil Collins, but this lead seems implausible given Collins' fame and distinctive musical style, which is drum-heavy and distinct from the song in question. Others speculated a possible connection to Newgrounds, akin to the song "Paragon," but this theory conflicts with Konstantinos' account of its Greek disco tape origins. The search, filled with speculation and intrigue, continues with no significant leads yet unveiled.

Chapulin Opening BGM

Chapulin Opening BGM, also referred to as "BGM Chapulin 1993" or the "Chapolin Polka," this musical riddle has baffled enthusiasts for decades. Its enigmatic 30-second snippet, a staple in the Brazilian-exclusive opening of the Mexican comedy TV series "Chapulin Colorado" since 1993 and featured in the show's promotions, continues to mystify.

Enter the realm of SBT (Sistema Brasileiro de Televisão), Brazil's media giant and the second-largest network, established in 1981. Known for their eclectic audio choices in the 1980s, SBT often infused its programming with a blend of instrumental snippets from commercial records and international library music. The "Chapulin Opening BGM" made its debut amidst this creative chaos, first surfacing in a cartoon block in the mid-80s, though whispers of earlier appearances linger unconfirmed.

Fast forward to 2022, when dedicated fans made a breakthrough. Connecting with an SBT sound department employee via Instagram, they unearthed a crucial revelation. The employee disclosed in a video that SBT's sound database only housed the known 30-second piece of the track, and its original title had vanished into the annals of history, leaving fans both intrigued and frustrated in their quest for answers.

The earliest known appearance of the enigmatic "Chapulin Opening BGM" is a moment captured in a children's cartoon frame. In this fascinating discovery, made in 2023 on Discord, the tune accompanies a vignette right before the launch of the cartoon Speedy Gonzales.

The year 2022 marked a poignant turn in the tune's history. Following the death of a renowned comedian from the sketch comedy show "Veja o Gordo," fans stumbled upon this unique tune playing in the background of a 1988 segment. Amidst the noise, a few additional seconds of the melody emerged, including a fleeting clarinet solo.

Flashback to the late 1980s: The tune finds a new home, becoming synonymous with the "Chapulin" sister-series "Chaves," prominently featured in the show's promotions.

1993 saw the debut of the sitcom "Chapulin Colorado," which adopted this enigmatic tune as its unofficial theme. For 26 years, it echoed daily across Brazil, becoming an iconic melody for generations of children and adults alike. Its mysterious origin continues to captivate fans, fueling their anticipation for its identification.

The decade-long quest to unravel the tune's origin often pointed to Jean-Jacques Perrey, but this assumption was debunked by the diligent community. Fans meticulously analyzed and identified over 500 songs related to the original audio and dub of the series in their search for answers.

The lead instrument, often thought to be a Moog synthesizer, remains a subject of debate. Its 'wobbly' and unstable sound suggests it might not be a synthesizer after all, but perhaps another instrument played with an unknown pedal effect. Enthusiasts suggest focusing on the tune's unique blend of clarinet and drum machine in their ongoing quest to demystify this captivating musical piece.

Markovian Parallax Denigrate

S pam, that notorious and ever-persistent digital nuisance, bombards the internet daily with millions of unsolicited messages. These range from the ridiculous – promises of instant weight loss or extravagant financial opportunities from distant lands – to the more familiar enticements of enhancing one's physical attributes in absurd ways. This relentless flood of spam is not just a modern phenomenon; it has a history of transforming the web into a bizarre landscape of unintentional humor and strange poetry.

Back in the days of the fledgling internet, particularly in the Usenet community of 1996, an event occurred that elevated spam to an almost artistic, surreal level. The infamous 'Markovian Parallax Denigrate' spam was a standout. This wasn't your average, run-of-the-mill spam. Each post under this cryptic title was a cascade of seemingly nonsensical words – a bewildering mix of references and phrases that hinted at a strange, almost deliberate intelligence behind them. Words like 'jitterbugging,' 'Newtonian,' and 'morphine napkin' jumbled together in an incomprehensible yet oddly fascinating stream.

On August 5, 1996, hundreds of these cryptic messages flooded Usenet groups, sparking a flurry of speculation and investigation among the platform's users – many of whom were academics and tech enthusiasts. They delved into the mystery with the kind of fervor and analytical rigor you would expect from such a community. Yet, despite their efforts, the enigma of these messages remained unsolved, adding to the lore of the early internet.

As the World Wide Web continued to grow and evolve, consuming more and more of the world's attention and cultural output, this peculiar incident was largely forgotten. Washed away in the ever-growing tide of information, it became a footnote in the history of the internet. Yet, it remains a fascinating glimpse into a time when the digital world was still wild and uncharted, a place where even spam could briefly touch the realms of the absurd and the artistic.

Around the mid-2000s, the peculiar incident of the 'Markovian Parallax Denigrate' spam messages resurfaced, this time in the realm of digital folklore. The event, which had remained a curious but obscure chapter in the history of the early internet, gained renewed attention when its Wikipedia page became a highlight on various lists of eerie and unexplained phenomena circulating on blogs and niche web forums. This renewed interest led to a deeper dive into the mystery, unearthing details that were even more intriguing and perplexing than the original spam messages.

Intrigued bloggers and digital sleuths made a significant discovery in the public Usenet archives hosted by Google. Among the remnants of the 'Markovian Parallax Denigrate' incident, only a single message survived, but it bore a subject line that echoed the mystery: "Markovian Parallax Denigrate." What truly caught the attention of these internet detectives was the email address of the sender – it was linked to a name well-known among national security circles: Susan Lindauer.

Lindauer, a former journalist, had gained notoriety in 2004 following her arrest under the accusation of acting as an agent for Saddam Hussein's Iraqi government. By the time of this discovery, she had become known for advocating various conspiracy theories, ranging from alleged cover-ups surrounding the Lockerbie bombing to promoting 9/11 truther narratives.

The discovery of Lindauer's connection to the 'Markovian Parallax Denigrate' message sparked a flurry of speculation. But just as the online community began piecing together this bizarre puzzle, the Wikipedia page detailing the incident mysteriously vanished. This abrupt disappearance did little to quell the growing whispers of conspiracy theories. Observers couldn't help but wonder if there was more to the story than met the eye. Was this spam message a covert communication, a coded message hiding a deep-seated government secret?

This twist in the tale transformed what was once a forgotten piece of internet history into a complex narrative involving two Susan Lindauers – the actual person and the enigmatic sender of the Usenet message. This convergence of identities breathed new life into one of the internet's oldest and most enigmatic mysteries, blurring the lines between digital folklore and real-world intrigue. The Markovian Parallax Denigrate, once a mere spam message, had evolved into a symbol of the internet's ability to intertwine reality and myth, creating a narrative that continues to captivate and perplex.

Susan Lindauer's life story is as complex and enigmatic as the infamous 'Markovian Parallax Denigrate' is to the realm of linguistic coherence. Her journey, far from the ordinary American narrative, is steeped in a series of unusual and intricate twists, becoming more labyrinthine upon closer inspection.

Her story begins in the chilly environs of Anchorage, Alaska. Here, she was raised in a family deeply rooted in the newspaper industry. Her father, John Howard Lindauer II, was a significant figure in Alaskan politics, having been a Republican nominee for governor. His 1998 gubernatorial campaign imploded amidst allegations of illegal campaign financing, adding a dramatic chapter to the family's history. Susan's mother, known for her penchant for wearing black capes, cut a striking figure in Anchorage, often perceived as a cosmopolitan, globe-trotting presence by the local community. This portrayal was notably captured in a feature by the Anchorage Daily News following Lindauer's eventual arrest.

At East Anchorage High School, Susan Lindauer was a study in contrasts.

Her classmates recalled her as both exceptionally intelligent and somewhat rebellious—a 'wild child'. Excelling academically, she had a strong affinity for the performing arts, reveling in the spotlight and the attention it brought. This blend of academic prowess and a flair for drama led her to pursue an impressive educational journey. After earning her bachelor's degree from Smith College, she attended the prestigious London School of Economics, where she completed a master's degree in public policy.

Her career began with journalism, where she worked for notable publications such as the Seattle Post-Intelligencer and US News and World Report. Leveraging her journalistic experience, she transitioned into the world of political communication, becoming a spokesperson in political circles. By 2004, Lindauer had established herself in Washington, D.C., rubbing shoulders with influential figures and discussing national intelligence—a topic of great interest in her network. Her political connections were noteworthy; she was even related to Andrew Carr, the chief of staff to President George W. Bush, and had worked with high-profile politicians like Democratic Senator Carol Moseley Braun of Illinois.

Despite her escalating professional success and the accumulation of powerful connections, there were signs that not everything was as it seemed with Lindauer. Those who knew her observed peculiarities in her behavior. Her colleagues at the Seattle Post-Intelligencer remembered her for unpredictable mood swings and erratic conduct. An incident involving quirky phone calls she allegedly made to a local merchant, asking them to cast spells on a rival newspaper, became a topic of workplace anecdotes.

In Washington, Lindauer was known by the moniker "Snowflake," a nickname that seemingly referred both to her Alaskan origins and her erratic behavior. Paul Hoven, a friend who claimed to have coined the name, succinctly explained its dual meaning to the New York Times Magazine: a reference to her Alaskan roots and a nod to her perceived eccentricity.

Susan Lindauer's journey is a complex tapestry of political activism, mysterious liaisons, and controversial claims, making her life story as intricate and enigmatic as the 'Markovian Parallax Denigrate' is to conventional linguistics. Her vehement opposition to sanctions against Middle Eastern countries was a prominent feature of her political stance. Lindauer's impassioned views propelled her into a self-appointed role of an intermediary, engaging in meetings with leaders from Muslim nations such as Libya and Iraq. She saw herself as a pivotal figure in Middle Eastern geopolitics, believing in her role as a "CIA asset" responsible for clandestine negotiations with Iraqi officials.

Lindauer's self-perception was grandiose, as evidenced in a 2002 letter addressed to President George W. Bush. In this correspondence, she described herself as an "expert in counterterrorism and peacemaking," boasting a unique and, in her words, "regrettably extraordinary gift for counterterrorism." She claimed to have accurately predicted numerous bombings and assassination attempts on world leaders.

Intriguingly, both Lindauer's brother and a close friend recalled her cautioning them to avoid New York City prior to the 9/11 attacks, adding a layer of mystery to her narrative. During the mid-1990s, coinciding with the 'Markovian Parallax Denigrate' event, Lindauer alleged that her "CIA handler," a businessman named Richard Fruisz, was privy to the true perpetrator behind the 1988 Pan Am Flight 103 bombing over Lockerbie, Scotland, which resulted in 270 fatalities. While the U.S. government attributed this act to the Libyan government, alternative theories at the time pointed towards Syrian-based terrorists. It wasn't until 2003 that the Libyan government officially acknowledged its role in the tragedy.

The complexity of Lindauer's story deepened with her arrest on March 11, 2004, at her home in Tacoma Park, Maryland. The FBI charged her with acting as an "unregistered agent of a foreign government," referencing a trip she made to Baghdad in 2002 during which she allegedly received $10,000. Despite her insistence on being a CIA operative, Lindauer contended that her arrest, facilitated under the Patriot Act, was a ploy to prevent her from disclosing the "truth" about 9/11. In her version of events, she portrayed the 9/11 hijackings as a facade for a controlled demolition of the World Trade Center and Building 7, and claimed that 9/11 terrorist Mohammed Atta was, in fact, a CIA agent.

Lindauer's saga took another turn in 2006 when a federal judge deemed her unfit for trial, citing mental health issues including paranoia and delusional thinking. A government psychiatrist reported that Lindauer claimed super-natural abilities and even an encounter with Osama bin Laden, during which he supposedly revealed a bomb's location, as noted in The New York Times.

Given these bewildering and dramatic elements in Lindauer's life, it's hardly surprising that when internet users stumbled upon her connection to the 'Markovian Parallax Denigrate' on Wikipedia, the conspiracy theories began to whirl. The blending of her controversial political activities, mysterious international connections, and her own claims of covert operations fed into a perfect storm of intrigue and speculation, igniting the imaginations of those delving into the depths of internet mysteries. Lindauer's story, woven with threads of political drama, alleged espionage, and mental health struggles, presented a narrative as compelling and convoluted as any spy novel, leaving many to ponder the blurred lines between truth and fiction in her extraordinary life.

Before the World Wide Web became a ubiquitous part of our lives, there existed a pioneering platform that laid the groundwork for much of today's online culture: Usenet. Conceived in 1980 by Duke University graduate students Tom Truscott and Jim Ellis, Usenet was an innovative network that connected computers via phone lines, allowing users to engage in discussions across a diverse range of topics. These discussions were organized into 'newsgroups', each dedicated to a particular subject, varying from atheism to current news, to sex advice. This early digital forum was a melting pot of internet culture, giving birth to now-familiar concepts such as emoticons, FAQs, and even the very notion of 'spam'—both the term and the phenomenon. When Tim

Berners-Lee was ready to introduce the World Wide Web to the world, he chose Usenet as his platform.

By 1996, Usenet had evolved into the world's de facto public bulletin board, a sprawling digital landscape where anyone could share a message with an international audience. If someone wanted to discreetly broadcast a clandestine message, Usenet was the ideal venue.

In the vast digital archive of Usenet maintained by Google, only one message titled 'Markovian Parallax Denigrate', sent from the email address susan_lindauer@worf.uwsp.edu, survives from August 5, 1996. However, this is just the tip of the iceberg. Records show that there were 52 other messages posted on the same day, each containing a similarly jumbled text and the words "Markovian," "parallax," and "denigrate" within their content. This suggests the possibility of a much larger, more complex pattern, potentially involving numerous additional messages now lost to time.

Google's archive of Usenet posts, which dates back to 1981, is not entirely comprehensive, especially in terms of spam content. According to a company representative, various factors, from privacy settings to issues of spam and abuse, have resulted in gaps in the historical record.

My stepfather, a devoted Usenet user during its heyday, was working at Cornell University's Theory Center, a hub for supercomputing, at the time of the 'Markovian Parallax Denigrate' event. He recollects the buzz and wild speculation that surrounded these mysterious postings. His impression was that the consensus among the Usenet community leaned towards the theory that this was a sort of intellectual exercise or proof-of-concept by some of the more intellectually gifted members of the Usenet community. The absence of any concrete follow-up or attribution to these messages seemed to reinforce the idea that this enigmatic event was ultimately harmless, a digital curiosity rather than something more sinister.

This perspective aligns with the nature of Usenet at the time—a space frequented by tech-savvy individuals, many of whom enjoyed pushing the boundaries of what could be achieved in this nascent digital environment. The 'Markovian Parallax Denigrate' incident, with its cryptic messages and elusive origins, fits into this context as a possible experiment or demonstration by the coding and intellectual elite of the Usenet community.

In the mid-1980s, a novel character named Mark V. Shaney, the brainchild of Rob Pike and Brad Ellis, made an unexpected entrance into the Usenet forum "net.singles." This forum served as a gathering place for individuals seeking companionship, often characterized by their shared experiences of solitude and unsuccessful romantic endeavors. Mark V. Shaney, whose name was a playful nod to the mathematical concept of a Markov Chain, was not your typical forum participant. This Markov Chain process informed the unique way in which he communicated: by producing text that was grammatically coherent but logically nonsensical, resembling a jumbled imitation of human language.

The truth behind Mark was both intriguing and innovative: he was a bot, an early experiment in artificial intelligence and natural language processing.

This peculiar invention caught the attention of 'Scientific American', which in 1989 offered an explanation of how Mark operated: The program would first absorb existing text, essentially 'studying' someone else's work. Then, it would generate its own text – a disjointed, rambling commentary that lacked logical sense but maintained linguistic structure. The magazine likened Mark's output to the remnants of understanding left in the mind of a distracted student after a marathon study session, or perhaps to the confused thoughts of a literature professor under the influence of mescaline.

A typical post from Mark in 1985 showcased this bizarre, almost surreal style of communication:

"It really galls me! I got a BA in computer science instead of a _Finnegan's Wake_! Did you really intend your posting to be able to improve one's life, and to win admiration — only the second seems to matter in schools? Granted, this clown may be the exception rather than the rule. It seemed that the intellectuals are usually the first to be so totally off the wall?"

The presence of Mark V. Shaney on the net.singles boards sparked a variety of reactions. Some perceptive readers quickly deduced that Mark was a computer-generated construct, a product of clever programming rather than a human being. However, many others were convinced that Mark was a real, albeit somewhat peculiar, individual. This divergence in perception underscored the bot's convincing mimicry of human speech patterns, albeit in a fragmented and often illogical way. Mark V. Shaney, in his own unique and quirky manner, blurred the lines between human and artificial communication, leaving a lasting impression on the early online community.

Rob Pike, who has since become a distinguished engineer at Google, shared insights with the Daily Dot about the motivations behind the creation of the Mark V. Shaney bot, which he developed alongside Brad Ellis. Pike explained that the bot was a product of their fascination with post-modernist pranks, a playful yet intricate exploration of the internet's possibilities. At the time, the philosophical works of Jacques Derrida, particularly his concept of deconstructionism, were gaining popularity among a niche group of literarily inclined computer enthusiasts. Derrida's deconstructionism posited that texts contain multiple, often conflicting meanings rather than presenting a unified, coherent message. Mark V. Shaney embodied this philosophy by disassembling and reassembling texts, placing words into new and often absurd contexts, thereby challenging the conventional understanding of language and meaning. Operating the prank manually would have been a laborious endeavor, but the bot efficiently managed it in mere minutes each day.

This context brings us to the enigmatic 'Markovian Parallax Denigrate', which bears a striking resemblance to the kind of message a bot using Markov Chains might generate — the clue is in the name itself. The question arises: was it simply another elaborate internet prank, or did it have a more profound purpose?

For those inclined to see clandestine patterns in everyday occurrences, the 'Markovian Parallax Denigrate' was more than just digital noise. Various theories have been proposed regarding its purpose and origins. Some speculated it was a coded message or a cipher, akin to the mysterious shortwave radio number stations historically used by intelligence agencies for covert communication. Others believed it was part of a disinformation campaign, deliberately linking Susan Lindauer's name to the emails as a smear tactic in response to her efforts to uncover the true perpetrator of the Lockerbie bombing. This theory gained traction particularly through a detailed exposition by the blog Rigorous Intuitions in 2006.

According to this viewpoint, certain parties, disturbed by Lindauer's probing into the murky waters of the Lockerbie incident, might have seen the 'Markovian Parallax Denigrate' as a tool for immediate disruption and a potential long-term strategy. The theory suggested that the mysterious posts were created to cast aspersions on Lindauer, insinuating her involvement in a duplicitous game and laying groundwork for future accusations, should the need arise.

In the web of conjecture and hypothesis surrounding the 'Markovian Parallax Denigrate', Lindauer was seen as a target, pursued by unseen forces. These theories, although unproven and verging on the hallucinatory, reflect the deep suspicion and intrigue that Lindauer's actions and subsequent narrative had ignited. In this complex web of speculation, the line between reality and delusion became increasingly blurred, with Lindauer at the center of a digital and real-world drama.

The emergence of grandiose theories on platforms like Usenet and the broader Internet is hardly surprising. These digital spaces have evolved into more than just arenas for elaborate post-modernist pranks. They've transformed the nature of information dissemination, making it inexpensive and universally accessible. For the first time in history, individuals from distant corners of the globe, from New Zealand to Tacoma Park, Maryland, could instantly connect over shared obsessions, be it lighthearted interests like cats and video games or more ominous topics such as elaborate world domination plots.

The Internet, with its myriad forums and blogs, became a fertile breeding ground for conspiracy theories. These digital echo chambers allowed such theories to not only take root but to flourish and spread at an unprecedented pace.

Damien Thompson, in his book "Counterknowledge: How We Surrendered to Conspiracy Theories, Quack Medicine, Bogus Science, and Fake History," highlights a paradox of the modern age. He points out that the legacy of the Enlightenment, grounded in meticulous measurement and observation of the material world, is now under threat, ironically due to the very scientific advances that have provided us with almost limitless access to information — information that is not always accurate or truthful.

A prime example of this phenomenon is the rise of 9/11 trutherism, which gained significant momentum through the Internet. The documentary "Loose Change," released in 2005, played a pivotal role in spreading the 9/11 truther narrative. Utilizing questionable evidence, it presented a case that quickly caught fire on platforms like YouTube, eventually selling over a million copies on DVD. Vanity Fair even went as far as to dub it potentially the "first Internet blockbuster."

This trend continued with figures like Robert Steele, Amazon's former top nonfiction reviewer, who carved out a reputation through his enthusiastic endorsements of 9/11 truther literature, including Susan Lindauer's 2010 book "Extreme Prejudice." In a five-star review, Steele speculated dramatically about the dangers Lindauer might have faced in prison, embodying the kind of sensationalism that often accompanies conspiracy narratives.

The Internet, in essence, acts as a colossal amplifier, magnifying and spreading ideas, both rational and irrational. Don DeLillo, in his novel "Underworld," described by some as the "chief shaman of the paranoid school of fiction," captures this phenomenon through the character of Sister Edgar. She becomes entranced by the boundless connections and knowledge of cyberspace, feeling engulfed by its systems and sensing the web's inherent paranoia.

Sister Edgar's experience is emblematic of many who navigate the Internet's vast and intricate network. It's a realm where connections are endless, where everything seems interlinked, and where, in the midst of this digital labyrinth, individuals can find others who share their most profound fears, beliefs, and suspicions. In this virtual world, ideas, especially those on the fringe, find fertile ground to grow and resonate with others who feel the same, creating communities bound together by shared narratives, no matter how far-fetched they may seem.

The theories surrounding Susan Lindauer and the Markovian Parallax Denigrate are undeniably intriguing. They seem to weave together seamlessly, suggesting a complex narrative. However, this intricate tapestry unravels upon closer inspection, particularly when considering the involvement of Susan Lindauer, the woman arrested in 2004. She herself has denied any connection to the mysterious message.

In an email exchange on October 10, Lindauer clarified her position: "I've heard of this cyber phenomenon, but I am not the Susan Lindauer who authored the code. Wish I could enlighten you. I'm baffled, too!"

This revelation shifts the focus to another Susan Lindauer, whose email address was linked to the Markovian Parallax Denigrate spam. Distinguishing between the two Susan Lindauers requires some internet sleuthing skills, particularly given the prominence of the Susan Lindauer involved in the 2004 arrest. A key clue lies in the email address associated with the Markovian Parallax Denigrate: susan_lindauer@worf.uwsp.edu.

This leads to the possibility that Mursau's email address was merely one among many academic emails harvested and utilized in the creation of the Markovian Parallax Denigrate messages, a common tactic to disguise the true origin of spam.

It's also worth considering the broader impact of such spam events on Usenet. Brad Templeton, an expert on the history of Usenet spam, described how the network was overwhelmed by spam in the mid-1990s, leading to its decline. This deluge of unwanted messages sparked intense debates within the Usenet community, caused users to hide their email addresses, and eventually drove many people away from the platform.

In the case of the Markovian Parallax Denigrate, the simplest explanation might be the most plausible: it could have been the work of a troll or prankster, or possibly an innocuous experiment with a Markov Chain by a programmer.

Yet, the allure of the unknown and the mysterious remains potent. The idea that the world's deepest secrets could be concealed within a spam folder is a tantalizing thought, adding a layer of intrigue and mystery to the mundane aspects of our digital lives.

Sad Satan

"Sad Satan" emerged in 2015 as a mysterious, horror-themed video game for Microsoft Windows, shrouded in an aura of creepypasta lore. In this eerily atmospheric game, players find themselves navigating through dimly lit, oppressive corridors from a first-person perspective. As they journey through this unsettling environment, their senses are assaulted by a series of unlicensed audio clips, adding to the game's disconcerting ambiance. This sensory experience is intermittently disrupted by sudden, full-screen images that flash across the screen, further intensifying the game's haunting atmosphere.

The game eschews traditional gameplay elements; there are neither defined goals nor victory conditions, leaving players to wander aimlessly in its shadowy world. The intrigue surrounding "Sad Satan" was amplified by a compelling backstory suggesting it was discovered on the dark web, with the enigmatic "ZK" being credited as its developer.

The enigma of "Sad Satan" first caught public attention through a video posted on the YouTube channel Ikenna Comics on June 25, 2015. This initial exposure sparked a flurry of interest, as English-language media outlets rapidly picked up the story, followed by international coverage. This widespread fascination fueled speculation that the game was engineered as a promotional tool for the YouTube channel.

Despite its notoriety, the version of "Sad Satan" featured in the Obscure Horror

Corner video was never officially released. Instead, a cloned version of the game began circulating, containing content that differed from the original. This subsequent version further contributed to the mystery and allure of "Sad Satan," cementing its place as a peculiar and enigmatic footnote in the history of horror-themed video gaming.

The original version of "Sad Satan," as showcased in the Obscure Horror Corner video, offers a unique and disturbing gameplay experience. Rendered in a first-person perspective, the game features deliberately blurred, monochromatic graphics that create an unsettling atmosphere. As players navigate through the eerie corridors, the game bombards their senses with a cacophony of audio samples. These samples are layered and looped, crafting a disorienting auditory landscape.

A significant aspect of the game's audio design leans on chilling recordings, including interviews with infamous murderers like Charles Manson. The game also uses distorted or reversed audio clips, adding a layer of surrealism to the experience. For instance, the opening features a reversed rendition of the song "I Love Beijing Tiananmen." Additionally, players encounter distorted clips from the Swedish Rhapsody numbers station, contributing to the game's cryptic and unnerving aura.

The theme of child abuse is a disturbing undercurrent in "Sad Satan." This is exemplified by the inclusion of The Doors' rendition of "Alabama Song," particularly the verse "Show me the way to the next little girl." This choice of audio is a haunting reminder of the game's dark themes.

As players control their character through the shadowy hallways, the game intermittently confronts them with images that dominate the screen, halting their progress. These images, often referencing child abuse, include depictions of figures implicated in Operation Yewtree, such as Jimmy Savile and Rolf Harris surrounded by children. Other images delve into themes of crime and include convicted or accused murderers like Tsutomu Miyazaki. Additionally, the game features photographs of Lady Justice statues, Colombian footballer Andrés Escobar, and political figures like former UK Prime Minister Margaret Thatcher and assassinated US President John F. Kennedy. The inclusion of works by Roger Ballen and Walter Sanders adds another layer of artistic depth to the game's imagery.

In a stark contrast to these complex themes, the only other "characters" encountered in the game are children who stand motionless, offering no interaction with the player. In a climactic twist revealed in the final video posted by Obscure Horror Corner, one of these children starts following the player, inflicting "contact damage." With no means of self-defense or healing, this encounter seals the player's inevitable demise, underscoring the game's relentless and unforgiving nature. This culmination serves as a grim metaphor for the inescapable horrors that pervade the game's narrative.

The mysterious origins of "Sad Satan" add an intriguing layer to its already enigmatic presence in the gaming world. In a revealing interview with Kotaku, the proprietor of the Obscure Horror Corner YouTube channel, known only as "Jamie," delved into how they stumbled upon this perplexing game. Jamie recounted discovering "Sad Satan" through a Tor hidden service, a discovery that was prompted by a tip-off from an anonymous subscriber. This subscriber themselves had allegedly found the link on a dark web internet forum, where it was shared by a user cryptically identified as "ZK."

This narrative of discovery, however, was met with skepticism among some followers of the game. Concerns arose that the game might include disturbing content, such as gore or child pornography. Addressing these fears, the Obscure Horror Corner owner assured that "Sad Satan" contained no such material, seemingly putting to rest some of the community's apprehensions.

The plot thickened following the Kotaku interview. The creation of a subreddit, "/r/sadsatan," dedicated to discussing the game, led to a startling revelation. The .onion address provided by Obscure Horror Corner for the game was scrutinized and found to contain invalid characters, casting doubt on the veracity of the game's origins. Merely three days later, a subsequent interview with the Obscure Horror Corner owner appeared on Kotaku. In a dramatic turn, it was claimed that the incorrect link was provided intentionally. The reason given was shocking: the game did, in fact, contain the graphic material previously denied, and Jamie did not want to bear the responsibility of spreading such content.

Patricia Hernandez, the original interviewer for Kotaku, later added an update to the article reflecting on these developments. She expressed regret for not approaching the story of "Sad Satan's" discovery with greater skepticism, acknowledging that while the article did hint at the game's more mythical than tangible existence, it fell short in clearly distinguishing between the concrete aspects of Jamie's story and those that were more speculative.

The "Sad Satan" saga marked the end of an era for the Obscure Horror Corner. This game was the last to be covered by the channel, which has since fallen into inactivity. This has led to speculation among the gaming community that "Sad Satan" might have been a creation of the Obscure Horror Corner itself, crafted as a clever ruse to boost the channel's viewership and subscriber count. This theory adds yet another layer to the mystery and intrigue that surrounds this infamous game.

Unfavorable Semicircle

"Unfavorable Semicircle" emerged as a mysterious enigma in the digital world, primarily through its YouTube channel, which became a focal point of intrigue and speculation. Launched on March 30, 2015, this enigmatic channel immediately caught attention with its relentless posting schedule, uploading two to three videos every couple of minutes. This unorthodox approach resulted in tens of thousands of videos, varying dramatically in duration from mere seconds to extensive eleven-hour marathons. Each video presented an abstract visual tableau, often accompanied by silence or a backdrop of distorted voices and bizarre auditory elements, crafting an ambiance of mystery and surrealism.

The channel's obscurity and unconventional content sparked widespread curiosity, escalating dramatically when one of its videos surfaced on Reddit. This exposure catapulted "Unfavorable Semicircle" into the limelight, eventually catching the attention of mainstream news outlets.

The enigmatic YouTube channel "Unfavorable Semicircle" commenced its peculiar journey in the digital realm on April 5, 2015, captivating a growing audience with its cryptic and unconventional video uploads. These uploads, typically just 5 seconds in duration, featured a man's voice articulating a single letter or number, set against a stark background punctuated by a solitary color pixel. Intriguingly, the majority of these videos bore titles starting with ↗, the astrological symbol for Sagittarius.

The channel's early phase was marked by videos named with seemingly random sequences of digits. This pattern evolved around February 14, 2016, when the channel began releasing a series titled "↗BRILL", each followed by a sequentially increasing number. These distinctive phases in the channel's content were later categorized into different "seasons" by early analysts.

The Unfavorable Semicircle phenomenon initially grew without any apparent efforts from the creator to seek attention. Yet, the sheer volume and bizarre nature of the videos naturally drew the curious eyes of the internet. Subreddits like r/UnexplainedPhotos and r/DeepIntoYouTube spotlighted these oddities, eventually leading to the creation of r/UnfavorableSemicircle, a dedicated community for unraveling the mystery.

The channel's growing notoriety caught the interest of bloggers and mainstream media alike, with noteworthy features on platforms like Atlas Obscura and BBC. The channel was rapidly becoming a viral sensation.

However, this burgeoning interest took an abrupt turn on February 25, 2016, at 15:40 EST, when YouTube suspended the Unfavorable Semicircle account for violating its Terms of Service, presumably due to the rapid rate of video uploads.

The suspension only fueled further fascination. The Reddit community intensified its investigations, spinning a web of theories and conjectures. On March 15, 2016, a breakthrough came with the discovery of garbled text on the Google+ page linked to the terminated YouTube account. This text led to the revelation of a Twitter account and a secondary YouTube channel, both named Unfavorable Semi. While several copycat channels surfaced, re-uploading the original videos, these accounts were recognized as the "official" continuation of the Unfavorable Semicircle narrative.

This period marked the beginning of what is referred to as the "modern era" of Unfavorable Semicircle. A deluge of new content was posted across YouTube and Twitter, featuring series with tens of thousands of videos, interspersed with unique, one-off creations.

The underlying purpose and meaning of these videos, however, remain shrouded in ambiguity. A significant discovery was that certain videos contained individual frames that, when assembled, formed larger, yet equally enigmatic images. The audio accompanying these videos is just as mysterious, ranging from distorted musical fragments to indistinct speech, and even sounds that some speculate could be encoded binary audio. Despite the extensive investigations and growing community interest, the intent behind Unfavorable Semicircle and the identity of its creator(s) remain among the internet's most compelling and unresolved mysteries.

The enigmatic saga of Unfavorable Semicircle took a dramatic turn on September 16, 2016, following a period of inactivity that had left its growing audience in suspense. This pause was broken by the emergence of a new YouTube channel named Stabilitory Newing, whose connection to Unfavorable Semicircle was hinted at in a post on the latter's Google+ page. Stabilitory Newing soon began uploading videos, echoing the distinct and cryptic style characteristic of UFSC, thus weaving another layer into the unfolding mystery.

Over the course of the next year, a series of revelations and discoveries further deepened the intrigue surrounding Unfavorable Semicircle:

1. An intricate analysis of the ↗HARVEST composite revealed small, legible text extracted from the introduction of the Wikipedia article on "Art", hinting at a deeper, possibly artistic, dimension to the project.
2. Some videos, such as ↗BREADTH, initially appeared to form mere color gradients in their regular composites. However, a deeper examination indicated these could be manipulated to extrapolate three-dimensional composites.
3. Enthusiasts embarked on efforts to reverse-engineer the UFSC process,

attempting to create videos that yielded composites akin to those of UFSC.

4. There was credible speculation that the peculiar glitches in UFSC videos were deliberate experiments to explore vulnerabilities like Stagefright and Rowhammer exploits in Android devices.

5. In an unexpected twist, the music in ↗RETIO was identified as Miss Patricola with the Virginians' 1922 recording of "Away Down East In Maine", adding a layer of historical context to the unfolding puzzle.

September 15, 2017, marked another pivotal moment in the UFSC narrative. After more than two months of silence, a new video titled ↗RESET STRANGE YD surfaced. This was quickly followed by the manual deletion of videos from the YouTube account, culminating in the account's termination. Simultaneously, the Stabilitory Newing YouTube and Twitter accounts were also deleted, seemingly by their operators.

Following this "reset", the only remaining vestige of UFSC's digital presence was its Google+ page, leaving the community pondering the implications of these abrupt changes.

In November 2017, the @unfavorablesemi Twitter account resurfaced, though it was unclear whether it was reactivated by the original UFSC creators or taken over by someone else. This account tweeted a cryptic text string, followed by a short video series and a standalone video. The community, while skeptical of the account's authenticity due to its deletion and reactivation, found the quality and consistency of the new content compelling enough to merit further investigation.

The plot thickened on New Year's Eve with yet another cryptic tweet. When decoded the next day, this message led to the discovery of a new YouTube channel, reigniting the flames of curiosity and speculation among followers.

In the shadow of the impending shutdown of Google+, a significant development unfolded in the mysterious saga of Unfavorable Semicircle. Observers noted the removal of the third post on the platform, which was soon replaced by a new, intriguing post titled "↗REAL". This post listed various accounts, implying that these were the authentic creations of the enigmatic UFSC's originators. Notably, the absence of the third YouTube channel from this list, coupled with a specific mention that the original Twitter account was authentic only up until the so-called "Reset", cast a shroud of doubt over the legitimacy of all videos posted after the Reset.

On December 31, 2019, the third YouTube channel, deemed "un-REAL" by the community, unexpectedly reemerged from a year-long hiatus. It broke its silence with the release of the first video in the ↗FORM series, marking the first activity since the cryptic final post on Google+.

In the wake of UFSC's diminished activity, the dedicated community of enthusiasts and investigators continued to convene on a Discord server. Although quieter than in its heyday, the server remained a hub for sharing new theories and findings. For instance, in June 2020, a notable discovery was made regarding the music in ↗DELOCK, identified as a distorted version of "Homesick" by Bailey's Lucky Seven. This revelation appeared to confirm and provide context to the previously enigmatic comment "HOMESICKDELOCK" found in the last Google+ post.

A significant development occurred on June 1, 2022, when the Unfavorable Semicircle Twitter account, @unfavorablesem, sprang to life for the first time since its creation in March 2019. In a flurry of activity, the account posted a series of tweets, including a quotation from the UFSC Discord server, what seemed to be more complete versions of various composites found in the BRILL series, as well as iterations of the ↗LOCK and ↗GOLDEN composites. Additionally, it shared a link to a song with accompanying commentary and extended an offer to answer questions from the community. However, it remained unclear whether the individual behind these tweets was indeed an original author of UFSC or someone who had taken control of the account.

Webdriver Torso

Webdriver Torso, an enigmatic YouTube channel, gained notoriety in 2014, sparking widespread curiosity and speculation about its mysterious nature. This intrigue was fueled by the channel's unique content and the playful jokes sprinkled within some videos.

The journey of Webdriver Torso began on March 7, 2013, when Google established the channel as part of an automated performance testing initiative. It started uploading videos on September 23, 2013, each featuring a sequence of simple slides paired with distinctive beeping sounds. These videos, seemingly mundane, captured the public's attention in 2014, leading to a flurry of theories and discussions among viewers who stumbled upon it. Notably, the channel deviated from its usual pattern with three unusual videos that contained jokes, further amplifying the public's fascination.

Despite the growing intrigue, the true purpose of Webdriver Torso remained shrouded in mystery, becoming a topic of popular discussion on the internet. The mystery endured until YouTube, with a touch of humor, finally revealed that the channel was indeed an internal tool for testing YouTube's performance and functionality.

The channel's activity, once prolific, saw a decline in the rate of video uploads. By May 4, 2017, Webdriver Torso had posted a staggering total of 624,774 videos. While its activity slowed down, the channel didn't go completely silent. It continued to sporadically post videos in May, August, and October of 2018, followed by additional uploads in July and October of 2019. The channel made a notable return with a video on November 22, 2021, followed by another post on May 3, 2022. In a surprising turn, 2023 saw a slight resurgence in activity, with five more videos being added to its vast collection. The story of Webdriver Torso, from its mysterious beginnings to its sporadic present-day activity, remains a fascinating chapter in the world of internet mysteries.

Despite the sheer volume of content, almost all the videos on Webdriver Torso adhered to a specific, enigmatic format. Each video, primarily 11 seconds in length, with some extending to 1, 5, or even 25 minutes, presented as slideshows. These slides, displayed for approximately one second each, featured a stark white background, upon which two solid-colored opaque rectangles – one red, the other blue – would appear. The sizes, shapes, and positions of these rectangles varied randomly, creating a seemingly endless array of combinations. Intriguingly, whenever these rectangles overlapped, the red always dominated, occasionally even completely obscuring the blue. Accompanying these visual elements was a series of random computer-generated wave tones, adding an auditory layer to the visual puzzle. The videos were labeled in a peculiar manner, with early uploads titled "aqua," later evolving to "tmp" followed by a series of random characters.

However, amidst this sea of formulaic uploads, three videos broke the mold, each adding to the Webdriver Torso enigma. One, humorously titled "tmpRkRL85," seemed ordinary until it revealed a silhouette of Rick Astley dancing in its latter half – a playful nod to the internet's Rickrolling phenomenon. Another, "00014," departed from the abstract slides to show a timelapse of the Eiffel Tower lighting up at night, ending with a brief glimpse of the Webdriver Torso Facebook page. The third, "0.455442373793," available exclusively in France for a fee, presented an episode of the American adult cartoon Aqua Teen Hunger Force dubbed in Spanish, an unusual deviation from the channel's standard content.

Adding to the intrigue, a video uploaded on May 3, 2022, titled "generated

10min vid," subtly differed in its labeling, diverging from the typical "aqua.flv" format to something more specific and detailed. These deviations from the norm, though few, added layers of mystery and speculation about the channel's purpose and the minds behind it.

After a hiatus following May 4, 2017, the channel briefly resumed uploads in May 2018, only to halt again shortly after. A curious incident occurred on November 16, 2020, when a video was uploaded and then quickly deleted, further fueling the enigma. As of the latest update, the most recent video from Webdriver Torso was posted on November 1, 2023.

Before YouTube officially acknowledged Webdriver Torso as a test channel, the internet was abuzz with various theories and speculations about its true purpose and identity. The enigmatic nature of the channel's content fueled a wide range of hypotheses, each more intriguing than the last. Some believed the channel was transmitting spy messages, a notion that aligned with the cryptic and formulaic nature of the videos. Others fancied the idea that the channel could be a means of communication by extraterrestrial life-forms, given the channel's seemingly otherworldly and inexplicable content.

A more grounded theory suggested that the videos were construction plans, perhaps a coded blueprint for something yet to be understood. Another fascinating hypothesis linked Webdriver Torso to Cicada 3301, a mysterious internet puzzle that had become synonymous with complex cryptography and recruitment of highly intelligent individuals. This theory gained traction among those who saw parallels between the cryptic nature of Cicada 3301 and the mysterious uploads on Webdriver Torso.

Despite Google's clarification that Webdriver Torso was merely a test channel, several aspects remained unexplained, particularly the humorous and seemingly out-of-place references in some videos. These included the inclusion of an episode from Aqua Teen Hunger Force, a Rick Astley silhouette, and time-lapse footage of the Eiffel Tower. Adding to the enigma was a cryptic comment made by the channel: "Matei is highly intelligent." The identity of this "Matei" sparked widespread speculation, with names like Basarab Matei, Matei Mancas, Matei Gruber, Matei Ciocarlie, and former Cinemassacre producer Mike Matei all being floated as possibilities. The intrigue deepened when this comment was later removed, adding another layer to the mystery.

The plot thickened when an Italian blogger, Soggetto Ventuno, discovered that Webdriver Torso was part of a network of accounts labeled "ytupload-testpartner_torso." Ventuno's investigations led to the uncovering of other accounts with similar video content, many of which were either pulled or made private following the publication of his findings. The network was linked to a Facebook page and a Twitter account, both of which were eventually taken down. The Facebook page had referenced Johannes Leitner, a Google Zürich employee, who was connected to another employee named Matei Gruber. This connection to "Matei" further fueled the speculations.

Ventuno's investigative work didn't stop there. He compared scenes from the pulled videos with photos of Google Zürich, finding striking similarities that suggested the videos were recorded at Google Zürich. This led to the conclusion that Webdriver Torso and similar channels were operated from this location.

The primary function of these videos was to test the quality of YouTube videos. After their creation, they were uploaded to YouTube, and then analyzed to determine the loss in quality post-upload.

When YouTube was questioned about Webdriver Torso, their response was a clever nod to one of the channel's anomalies: "We're never gonna give you uploading that's slow or loses video quality, and we're never gonna let you down by playing YouTube in poor video quality. That's why we're always running tests like Webdriver Torso." This statement, echoing the lyrics of Rick Astley's "Never Gonna Give You Up," not only confirmed the channel's purpose but did so with a playful reference to one of the internet's most enduring memes, encapsulating the curious and whimsical essence of the Webdriver Torso saga.

Chip-chan

"Chip-chan" is an enigmatic and mysterious figure from South Korea, whose true age remains unknown. She is known for her extraordinary claim of being implanted with a mind-control device and her allegations of being held captive by a corrupt police officer, whom she refers to as "P". Chip-chan has turned to the digital world for help, live-streaming her life from her apartment daily for over a decade, offering a window into her unusual existence.

This intriguing story began to unfold in 2008 when Chip-chan was first noticed in a webcam thread on 4chan. This online community is known for its members' exploration of various open-source webcams, sharing intriguing and unusual findings. Chip-chan caught the community's attention when she was spotted sleeping in an odd position, so peculiar that she was initially mistaken for deceased, sparking widespread curiosity and concern among the forum users. However, it was soon discovered that she was indeed alive, but her sleep patterns were far from normal—often sleeping for extraordinarily long periods at odd hours of the day, and in uncomfortable positions such as sitting in a chair or sprawled on the floor.

The mystery deepened when an anonymous user stumbled upon her Word-Press blog, which led to the discovery of several other blogs authored by Chip-chan. In these blogs, she detailed her distressing experience, claiming that a mind-control weapon had been implanted "at a cartilage bone 3cm off the anklebone." She also believed that she had a chip implanted under her left eyebrow. Her story, woven with elements of conspiracy, surveillance, and personal distress, has captivated a global audience, making her a subject of fascination and concern in the online community.

In the heart of her apartment, Chip-chan has established a unique and haunting digital presence through a network of webcams, which she seems to have installed herself. These cameras, offering a 24/7 live stream, reveal the intimate and often unsettling details of her life, where every room is adorned with handwritten signs in Korean. These visual cues are intertwined with an audio clip, narrated in her own voice, detailing the ominous narrative of "P", the alleged mind control weapon, and her harrowing circumstances.

The streams paint a vivid picture of Chip-chan's life, dominated by long hours spent surfing the web and sleeping, often exceeding 12 hours in a single stretch. Her appearance is one of neglect and deteriorating health, marked by extreme lethargy. Disturbingly, she occasionally exhibits skin rashes and unexplained wounds, which she documents through photos and videos, adding to the enigma surrounding her. This peculiar and isolated existence has been her reality since at least 1996.

Her narrative is one of entrapment and helplessness, dictated by the supposed chip implanted in her body. According to Chip-chan, this chip empowers its controller to render her unconscious at will, effectively confining her within her apartment. Yet, there are instances where she has been known to leave her apartment, and she has even changed residences on several occasions. Despite these movements, she refrains from seeking police intervention, fearing that it would alert the corrupt officer "P" to her actions. Instead, she appeals to her viewers for assistance in battling "P", urging them to spread her story and contact individuals like Park Sang-Man, her former landlord, for aid.

Interactions with Chip-chan are limited yet poignant. She engages with her audience through responses to emails and comments on her blogs, but curiously remains silent in the chat during her streams.

Over the years, Chip-chan's story has given rise to a multitude of theories, ranging from speculations of an elaborate art project, suggestions of mental illness, to the chilling possibility of her story being a grim reality. The online community's fascination with her situation has led to various attempts to reach out, including contacting local authorities and even personal visits to her home, each effort adding another layer to the complex and haunting tapestry of Chip-chan's life.

"P"

Park Sung-Dong, referred to as "P" in the unsettling narrative of Chip-chan, emerges as a central and enigmatic figure in her life. Allegedly a former police officer, "P" is depicted as the sinister mastermind behind Chip-chan's prolonged captivity. Now in his 60s, "P" reportedly retired in 2018, yet his shadow looms large in the tale spun by Chip-chan.

According to Chip-chan, it was "P" who, around 2006, implanted a VeriChip in her foot—a device that she believes grants him near-total control over her. This control, as per her claims, extends to an unnerving degree: manipulating her thoughts, inducing skin outbreaks, seeing the world through her eyes, and even rendering her unconscious at his whim. It's through these seemingly extraordinary powers that "P" allegedly keeps Chip-chan prisoner within the walls of her own home, exerting this control for the purpose of extortion.

In her blogs and live-streams, Chip-chan paints "P" as the arch-villain in her saga, the orchestrator of her suffering. She pleads with her viewers for assistance in thwarting "P", suggesting various means such as spreading awareness of her plight and reaching out to a person named Park Sang-Man to investigate her situation. Her distrust of the police, whom she believes to be corrupt, only intensifies her sense of isolation and desperation.

"P" isn't the only police officer Chip-chan mentions; her blog also references other officers, including Park Sung Dong and Ahan Byung Kuk, who she suspects are part of this broader conspiracy against her. She has documented encounters with local police in her area, particularly in the early 2010s, capturing these interactions in photographs as part of her ongoing effort to expose what she perceives as a vast and malevolent network.

This intricate web of allegations, fears, and pleas for help, centered around the figure of "P", forms the core of Chip-chan's distressing story—a narrative that blurs the lines between reality and paranoia, leaving her audience both captivated and concerned.

Verichip

The VeriChip, developed by Applied Digital Solutions, stands as a technological marvel in the realm of identification systems. This injectable chip, approximately the size of a rice grain, is designed to be inserted under the skin of humans or animals for biometric verification purposes. Comprising an identification number, an electromagnetic coil for data transmission, and a tuning capacitor, all these components are securely housed within a silicon and glass container that is biocompatible with human tissue. This chip operates on wireless transmission technology akin to the ID chips used in animal shelters for tagging pets, and it can be detected by a specialized scanner from a distance of up to four feet.

Initially, VeriChip was conceived as a medical tool, akin to a high-tech medical alert bracelet, providing critical information about a patient's medical history to healthcare professionals. However, its applications have since expanded beyond the medical realm to include security and automated data collection. The concept of a GPS-enabled VeriChip raises the tantalizing possibility of pinpointing an individual's location in terms of latitude, longitude, altitude, speed, and direction. In a scenario where such GPS implants are widespread, they could potentially enable authorities to locate missing persons, fugitives, or suspects fleeing crime scenes.

Yet, this technology is not without its detractors. Critics argue that it could be a tool for political oppression, enabling governments to track and persecute human rights defenders, labor activists, civil dissidents, and political adversaries. Furthermore, it raises concerns about personal safety, as criminals and domestic abusers could exploit such technology to stalk and harass their targets, and child predators could use it to track and abduct children.

Within this context of technological advancement and ethical debate, Chip-chan's story emerges. She asserts that a police officer, whom she refers to as "P", has implanted a VeriChip in her foot and eyebrow. According to her, this chip grants "P" the ability to manipulate her thoughts and control her consciousness, causing her to fall in and out of sleep abruptly. She also believes that this chip is responsible for her not having any dreams since 2008 and attributes various other health issues to its presence. This intersection of cutting-edge technology and Chip-chan's distressing narrative adds a layer of complexity and intrigue to her situation, blurring the lines between reality and perceived manipulation.

GhostNet

G hostNet, a term coined by the Information Warfare Monitor's team of researchers, represents a sophisticated and far-reaching cyber espionage network, unearthed in March 2009. This operation, believed to be tied to an advanced persistent threat - a stealthy network actor specializing in prolonged and undetected spying - primarily operates from within the People's Republic of China. Its extensive infiltration activities span across 103 countries, targeting high-profile political, economic, and media entities. Notably, GhostNet's cyber reach compromised systems in embassies, foreign ministries, other significant government offices, and even the Tibetan exile centers led by the Dalai Lama located in India, London, and New York City.

The uncovering of GhostNet was a result of a meticulous 10-month investigation by the Information Warfare Monitor (IWM), initiated after the Dalai Lama's representatives in Geneva expressed concerns about potential breaches in their network security. The IWM, comprising experts from The SecDev Group and Canadian consultancy along with the Citizen Lab at the Munk School of Global Affairs, University of Toronto, delved deep into this cyber mystery. Their groundbreaking findings were eventually published in the Infowar Monitor, an affiliated journal. Complementing this effort, researchers from the University of Cambridge's Computer Laboratory, backed by the Institute for Information Infrastructure Protection, also played a crucial role, particularly at one of the key investigation sites in Dharamshala, the home of the Tibetan government-in-exile.

The New York Times, on March 29, 2009, brought the existence and the intricate workings of 'GhostNet' to public attention. Initially, the investigators concentrated on the allegations of Chinese cyber espionage activities targeting the Tibetan exile community, scrutinizing incidents where sensitive email communications and other data were illicitly accessed and extracted. This extensive investigation into GhostNet not only unveiled a complex web of cyber surveillance but also highlighted the emerging threats in the digital era, where geopolitical tensions manifest in the realm of information technology and cyber warfare.

The intricate web of GhostNet's cyber espionage extended its reach to a diverse range of diplomatic missions and government offices, painting a complex picture of international cyber vulnerability. Among the compromised were the embassies of India, South Korea, Indonesia, Romania, Cyprus, Malta, Thailand, Taiwan, Portugal, Germany, and Pakistan, as well as the Prime Minister's office of Laos. This extensive breach also impacted the foreign ministries of numerous countries, including Iran, Bangladesh, Latvia, Indonesia, the Philippines, Brunei, Barbados, and Bhutan. Intriguingly, while there was no concrete evidence of infiltration into the governmental systems of the U.S. or the UK, a NATO computer was under surveillance for a significant half-day period, and the Indian embassy in Washington, D.C., was notably compromised.

Since its initial detection, GhostNet has not relented in its cyber assaults on global government networks. A striking example occurred in early 2011, when Canadian official financial departments were attacked, leading to a substantial offline period. While governments typically remain reticent about admitting to such cyber breaches, these incidents often come to light through verification by official yet anonymous sources.

The modus operandi of GhostNet's attacks is both sophisticated and insidious. Target organizations receive seemingly relevant emails, laced with malicious attachments. Once these attachments are opened, they unleash a Trojan horse, penetrating the system and establishing a connection to a control server, predominantly located in China. This breached system then becomes a puppet, executing commands issued by the remote control server. One such command frequently involves the downloading and installation of a specific Trojan known as Ghost Rat. This notorious malware grants attackers real-time, comprehensive control over computers running Microsoft Windows.

The capabilities of Ghost Rat are alarmingly extensive. It allows attackers not only to control or inspect the infected computer but also to activate camera and audio-recording functions, turning these devices into potent surveillance tools. This chilling aspect of GhostNet's operation underscores the evolving threats in the digital landscape, where privacy and security are constantly under siege by unseen and far-reaching cyber forces.

The investigation into GhostNet, spearheaded by the Information Warfare Monitor (IWM), unfolds like a complex cyber mystery, intertwining global politics, espionage, and cutting-edge technology. The researchers at IWM have carefully stated that direct evidence linking the Chinese government to the GhostNet spy network is lacking. However, in a striking contrast, a report from researchers at the University of Cambridge presents a different perspective, suggesting that the Chinese government might be behind the cyber intrusions they analyzed, particularly those at the Office of the Dalai Lama.

The plot thickens as researchers consider alternative theories about Ghost-Net's origins. Some speculate that it could be the brainchild of private Chinese citizens driven by profit motives or patriotic zeal. Others suggest that it might be an elaborate ruse crafted by intelligence agencies from other countries, such as Russia or the United States. Amidst these theories, the Chinese government's official stance is unequivocal, asserting a strict prohibition against any form of cybercrime.

The intrigue deepens with the "Ghostnet Report," which documents several infections unrelated to GhostNet at various Tibetan-related organizations. Scott J. Henderson, delving into the data provided by the IWM report, managed to trace one of the operators of a non-GhostNet infection back to Chengdu. This individual, identified as a 27-year-old man with connections to the Chinese hacker underground, is an alumnus of the University of Electronic Science and Technology of China.

While direct evidence implicating the Chinese government in the cyber attacks against Tibetan targets remains elusive, researchers at Cambridge have observed certain actions by Chinese officials that intriguingly align with the information obtained through computer intrusions. One notable instance involved a diplomat who faced pressure from Beijing following his receipt of an email invitation for a meeting with the Dalai Lama. Another incident saw a Tibetan woman interrogated by Chinese intelligence, who confronted her with transcripts of her online conversations. These transcripts could potentially have been obtained through surveillance of platforms like TOM-Skype, the Chinese version of Skype known for logging and storing text messages.

Adding another layer to this cyber espionage saga, IWM researchers have found that when detected, GhostNet is often controlled from IP addresses located on Hainan Island, China. This detail is particularly intriguing as Hainan hosts the Lingshui signals intelligence facility and the Third Technical Department of the People's Liberation Army. Moreover, one of the four control servers for GhostNet has been identified as a government server, although the specifics of this connection remain unclear.

This unfolding story of GhostNet not only highlights the complexities of cyber warfare and espionage but also raises profound questions about privacy, national security, and the shadowy interplay of global powers in the digital age.

Bitcoin's Founder

Satoshi Nakamoto stands as an enigmatic and pseudonymous figure, widely recognized as the mastermind behind the groundbreaking creation of Bitcoin. This individual or possibly a group of people not only conceptualized and penned the highly influential Bitcoin white paper but also spearheaded the development and deployment of Bitcoin's original reference implementation. In doing so, Nakamoto introduced the world to the first blockchain database, a technology that has since revolutionized the digital landscape.

Nakamoto's involvement with Bitcoin was active and pivotal until December 2010, after which the mysterious figure seemingly faded from the forefront of the cryptocurrency scene. This abrupt departure has fueled an ongoing wave of speculation and theories about the true identity of Satoshi Nakamoto. Despite Nakamoto's claim in 2012 of being a male resident of Japan, the clues surrounding this persona remain sparse and nebulous. As a result, the speculation has frequently centered around various individuals in the fields of software and cryptography, primarily based in the United States and Europe. This enduring mystery has only deepened the intrigue surrounding Satoshi Nakamoto, making this persona a subject of fascination and curiosity in the tech world and beyond.

The journey of Satoshi Nakamoto, is a tale woven with innovation, secrecy, and significant impact on the digital world. It all began in 2007 when Nakamoto set out to write the code for a new form of digital currency, an endeavor that would eventually reshape the landscape of financial transactions globally. In a pivotal moment on August 18, 2008, either Nakamoto or an associate took the significant step of registering the domain name bitcoin.org, laying the groundwork for a revolutionary new concept. This was swiftly followed by the creation of a website at the same address, signaling the first public emergence of Bitcoin.

The end of October 2008 marked a significant milestone in Nakamoto's journey. On October 31st, Nakamoto published a comprehensive white paper on the cryptography mailing list at metzdowd.com. This paper, titled "Bitcoin: A Peer-to-Peer Electronic Cash System," detailed an innovative approach to digital cryptocurrency. It served not only as a theoretical blueprint but also as a clarion call for a new era in digital finance.

The actual birth of Bitcoin occurred on January 9, 2009, when Nakamoto released version 0.1 of the Bitcoin software on SourceForge. This release was more than just a software launch; it was the inauguration of the Bitcoin network. Nakamoto mined the very first block of Bitcoin, known as the genesis block (block number 0), which contained a reward of 50 bitcoins. Embedded within this inaugural block was a message: "The Times 03/Jan/2009 Chancellor on brink of second bailout for banks." This text, referencing a headline from the UK newspaper The Times, is widely interpreted as a timestamp and a critical commentary on the instability of the fractional-reserve banking system.

Nakamoto's active involvement with Bitcoin's development continued until mid-2010. During this time, he was the sole custodian of the project, personally making all modifications to the Bitcoin source code. However, in a move that surprised many, Nakamoto then transferred control of the source code repository and the network alert key to developer Gavin Andresen. Along with this, he passed on several related domain names to key figures in the Bitcoin community, subsequently withdrawing from any recognized involvement in the project.

An intriguing aspect of Nakamoto's legacy is his Bitcoin holdings. Estimates suggest that Nakamoto owns between 750,000 and 1,100,000 bitcoins. In November 2021, when Bitcoin reached its peak value of over $68,000, this meant that Nakamoto's net worth could have been as high as $73 billion, positioning him among the world's wealthiest individuals. Despite this immense wealth, Nakamoto's identity and intentions remain shrouded in mystery, making him one of the most enigmatic figures in the modern technological era.

The persona of Satoshi Nakamoto, the enigmatic creator of Bitcoin, is shrouded in layers of mystery and speculation, especially regarding his personal identity and background. Throughout his engagement in the development and discussion of Bitcoin, Nakamoto was meticulously careful to never reveal any personal information. However, he occasionally shared his thoughts on topics such as banking and fractional-reserve banking, giving a glimpse into his possible interests and expertise.

In a rare instance of self-disclosure, Nakamoto's profile on the P2P Foundation website, as of 2012, declared him to be a 37-year-old male residing in Japan. This revelation, however, only fueled more speculation about his true identity, with many observers doubting his Japanese origin due to his seemingly native-level proficiency in English.

The theories about Nakamoto's true identity are diverse and intriguing. Dan Kaminsky, a renowned security researcher who meticulously examined the Bitcoin code, posited that Nakamoto might not be an individual, but rather a collective of people, or a singular genius of extraordinary capacity. Laszlo Hanyecz, a developer who interacted with Nakamoto via email, observed that the Bitcoin code was so sophisticated and well-constructed that it seemed unlikely to be the work of just one person. Gavin Andresen, another prominent figure in the Bitcoin community, also weighed in, describing Nakamoto's coding style as exceptionally brilliant yet idiosyncratic.

Adding to the mystery, the use of British English in both the source code comments and forum postings by Nakamoto sparked further theories. Phrases like "bloody hard," and British spellings such as "colour" and "grey," led some to speculate that Nakamoto, or at least one member of a group possibly representing him, might have origins in a Commonwealth country. Additionally, Nakamoto's citation of a headline from London's Times newspaper in the first-ever Bitcoin block hinted at a possible connection or interest in the British government.

A fascinating clue to Nakamoto's lifestyle and possibly his geographic location came from Stefan Thomas, a Swiss software engineer and active member of the Bitcoin community. Thomas analyzed over 500 of Nakamoto's forum posts and charted their timestamps. The data revealed a striking pattern: there was a significant drop in activity between 5 a.m. and 11 a.m. Greenwich Mean Time, corresponding to midnight to 6 a.m. Eastern Standard Time, and 2 p.m. to 8 p.m. Japan Standard Time. This suggested an unusual sleep pattern for someone purported to be living in Japan, as the quiet hours consistently included afternoons and early evenings in Japanese time. Remarkably, this pattern persisted even on weekends, further deepening the enigma of Nakamoto's true whereabouts and lifestyle. This meticulous analysis of Nakamoto's online activity patterns opened yet another intriguing chapter in the ongoing saga to uncover the identity behind the pseudonym Satoshi Nakamoto.

Hal Finney, was a notable figure in the history of cryptography and digital currency, particularly known for his significant contributions to the early development of Bitcoin. As a pioneering cryptographic expert, Finney was the very first individual, aside from the enigmatic Satoshi Nakamoto, to not only use the Bitcoin software but also to actively engage with it by reporting bugs and suggesting improvements. His involvement with Bitcoin during its nascent stages marked a critical moment in the evolution of this groundbreaking digital currency.

An intriguing twist in Finney's story involves his geographical proximity to a person named Dorian Satoshi Nakamoto. Forbes journalist Andy Greenberg noted that Finney lived just a few blocks away from this individual, sparking curiosity and speculation in the crypto community. In pursuit of uncovering the truth behind the real identity of Satoshi Nakamoto, Greenberg sought the expertise of the writing analysis consultancy Juola & Associates. They were tasked with comparing a sample of Finney's writing with that of Nakamoto's. The results were striking; Finney's writing bore the closest resemblance to Nakamoto's among all the candidates analyzed, which included suggestions by Newsweek, Fast Company, The New Yorker, Ted Nelson, and Skye Grey.

Greenberg subsequently proposed two theories: either Finney had ghostwritten on behalf of Nakamoto, or he had used his neighbor Dorian's identity as a cover for his online activities. However, upon personally meeting Finney, reviewing the email exchanges between him and Nakamoto, and examining the history of his Bitcoin wallet (which included the very first Bitcoin transaction from Nakamoto to Finney), Greenberg concluded that Finney's denials of being Nakamoto were credible. Notably, Juola & Associates also determined that Nakamoto's emails to Finney were more in line with Nakamoto's known writings than with Finney's.

The quest to unveil Nakamoto's identity took a dramatic turn with the publication of a high-profile article by journalist Leah McGrath Goodman in Newsweek on March 6, 2014. Goodman identified Dorian Prentice Satoshi Nakamoto, a Japanese American residing in California and born with the name Satoshi Nakamoto, as the potential creator of Bitcoin. Goodman's identification was based on a combination of circumstantial evidence: Nakamoto's professional background as a physicist and systems engineer, his libertarian views, and his encouragement of entrepreneurial independence from government control.

The most compelling moment came when Goodman, during an in-person interview, questioned Nakamoto about Bitcoin. His response, perceived as a tacit admission, was: "I am no longer involved in that and I cannot discuss it. It's been turned over to other people. They are in charge of it now. I no longer have any connection." This statement, however, was later subject to various interpretations.

The Newsweek article caused a media frenzy, with reporters swarming Dorian Nakamoto's residence and following him to an interview. In a significant development, the P2P Foundation account associated with the pseudonymous Nakamoto, which had been inactive for five years, posted a message stating: "I am not Dorian Nakamoto." This denial added yet another layer of mystery to the ongoing saga. In a comprehensive interview that followed, Dorian Nakamoto categorically denied any involvement with Bitcoin, claiming he had never even heard of the currency before the interview and had misunderstood Goodman's questions as pertaining to his past classified work or his tenure at Citibank.

Further complicating the narrative, the P2P Foundation account later posted another message, claiming it had been hacked. This revelation cast doubt on the authenticity of the earlier denial of Dorian Nakamoto's involvement.

One of the more compelling theories emerged in December 2013 when blogger Skye Grey used what he termed "stylometric analysis" to draw a connection between Nick Szabo and the Bitcoin white paper. Szabo, a well-known figure in the realm of decentralized currency and an early proponent of "bit gold," a precursor to Bitcoin, had long shown interest in pseudonymity, especially in the 1990s. This connection was further underlined by Szabo's own words in a May 2011 article where he acknowledged that only a few individuals, including himself, Wei Dai, and Hal Finney, were significantly engaged with the idea of a decentralized currency like Bitcoin until the appearance of Nakamoto.

Financial author Dominic Frisby also delved into this mystery, presenting a substantial amount of circumstantial evidence linking Szabo to Nakamoto, though he conceded the absence of definitive proof. Szabo himself has consistently denied being Nakamoto. In a July 2014 email to Frisby, Szabo brushed off the suggestion, stating he was accustomed to such misidentifications. In the journalistic sphere, Nathaniel Popper of The New York Times highlighted that the most persuasive evidence he encountered pointed to a reclusive American of Hungarian descent, Nick Szabo, as the real Nakamoto.

In another dramatic turn, on December 8, 2015, Wired magazine published an article suggesting that Australian academic Craig Steven Wright might either be the true inventor of Bitcoin or a masterful hoaxer. This claim was complicated by Wright's decision to delete his Twitter account and the lack of response to press inquiries from him and his ex-wife. On the same day, Gizmodo released a story claiming to possess evidence obtained by a hacker who had accessed Wright's email accounts. This evidence purported that Satoshi Nakamoto was a pseudonym used jointly by Craig Steven Wright and David Kleiman, a computer forensics analyst who had passed away in 2013. Wright's claim to be Nakamoto was later supported by notable figures in the Bitcoin community, including Jon Matonis, former director of the Bitcoin Foundation, and developer Gavin Andresen.

Wright provided a curious explanation for his choice of the pseudonym "Nakamoto." He claimed that the surname was chosen in homage to Tominaga Nakamoto, a Japanese philosopher, whom he learned about through his Japanese martial arts instructor. The first name "Satoshi" was inspired by a character from Pokémon, which Wright associated with the current financial system that, in his view, needed to be "burned to ash" to make way for cryptocurrency.

However, several prominent Bitcoin figures remained skeptical of these reports. Follow-up investigations raised the possibility that the evidence could be part of an elaborate hoax, a theory that even Wired admitted cast doubt on their initial suggestion that Wright was Nakamoto. Bitcoin developers like Peter Todd and Jeff Garzik expressed doubts about the cryptographic proof presented by Wright, with security researcher Dan Kaminsky labeling Wright's claims as potentially deceitful.

Wright's pursuit of recognition as Bitcoin's creator took a legal turn in May 2019 when he began using English libel law to sue individuals who denied his claim or labeled him a fraud. In a significant move in 2019, Wright registered US copyrights for the Bitcoin white paper and the Bitcoin 0.1 software code. His team asserted that this registration was an acknowledgment by a government agency of Wright's identity as Nakamoto. However, the United States Copyright Office issued a statement clarifying their role, emphasizing that they do not verify the legal ownership of a work but merely assess its eligibility for copyright. This clarification indicated that the ultimate determination of Nakamoto's true identity, if ever disputed in court, would remain a matter for legal adjudication rather than administrative copyright registration.

In a 2011 article in The New Yorker, journalist Joshua Davis embarked on a quest to unravel this mystery, zeroing in on several potential candidates. Among them were Dr. Vili Lehdonvirta, a Finnish economic sociologist known for his expertise in virtual economies, and Michael Clear, a cryptography student at Trinity College Dublin in 2008. Both individuals found themselves in the spotlight as potential creators of Bitcoin. However, each strongly refuted these claims, with Clear and Lehdonvirta unequivocally denying any involvement with the creation of Bitcoin.

In October 2011, the investigative pursuit took another turn when Adam Penenberg, writing for Fast Company, brought forth new circumstantial evidence. He suggested that Neal King, Vladimir Oksman, and Charles Bry could potentially be the individuals behind the Nakamoto pseudonym. This speculation was fueled by the trio's joint patent application filed in 2008, which notably contained the phrase "computationally impractical to reverse," a key phrase that also appeared in the Bitcoin white paper authored by Nakamoto. Adding to the intrigue, the domain name bitcoin.org was registered just three days after this patent application was filed. However, when Penenberg reached out to them, all three men categorically denied being

Nakamoto.

In May 2013, the speculation took a scholarly turn when Ted Nelson, a notable figure in the world of technology and philosophy, proposed a new candidate: Japanese mathematician Shinichi Mochizuki. Nelson's speculation was based on his analysis of Mochizuki's profound expertise and his low-profile demeanor. However, this theory was met with skepticism, and an article in The Age newspaper later reported that Mochizuki had denied these claims, though the source of this denial was not clearly attributed.

The narrative took yet another twist in a 2013 article published by Vice, which presented a different set of potential candidates for the Nakamoto identity. This time, the list included Gavin Andresen, a prominent figure in the Bitcoin community; Jed McCaleb, known for his involvement in the creation of several successful cryptocurrency platforms; and even an unnamed government agency.

In 2013, this ongoing quest saw a notable development when two Israeli mathematicians, Dorit Ron and Adi Shamir, put forward a hypothesis linking Nakamoto to Ross Ulbricht, the infamous figure behind the Silk Road marketplace. Their claim was based on a detailed analysis of the complex web of Bitcoin transactions. However, this theory was short-lived as they later retracted their claim, adding yet another twist to the enigmatic puzzle of Nakamoto's identity.

In 2016, the narrative took an interesting turn when the Financial Times posited that Nakamoto might not be a single individual but rather a collective of people. This group, according to the publication, could potentially include notable figures such as Hal Finney, a pioneering cryptographic engineer; Nick Szabo, known for his work on digital contracts and digital currencies; and Adam Back, the inventor of Hashcash, a system that laid the groundwork for Bitcoin's proof-of-work algorithm. The intrigue deepened in 2020 when the YouTube channel Barely Sociable released a claim suggesting that Adam

Back himself might be Nakamoto. However, Back firmly denied this assertion. Adding to the speculation, Charles Hoskinson, the founder of Cardano and a co-founder of Ethereum, expressed his view that Adam Back was a likely candidate for being Nakamoto.

Another surprising twist in the Nakamoto saga occurred when Elon Musk, the renowned entrepreneur and CEO of SpaceX and Tesla, found himself at the center of speculation. In a tweet dated November 28, 2017, Musk addressed and denied a claim made in a Medium post by a former SpaceX intern, which speculated that he might be the mysterious Bitcoin creator.

In 2019, journalist Evan Ratliff introduced a new and unexpected candidate into the Nakamoto narrative: Paul Le Roux, a notorious criminal figure known for drug trafficking. Ratliff's claim added a dark horse to the roster of potential Nakamotos, further complicating the search for the truth.

The year 2021 saw yet another development in this ongoing saga when developer Evan Hatch proposed a new name: Len Sassaman, a well-respected figure in the cypherpunk community and associated with the COSIC research group. This theory gained some traction in the Bitcoin community, especially considering that Sassaman had been mentioned on the bitcointalk forum as early as March 15, 2013, as a possible Satoshi Nakamoto.

Each of these claims, denials, and speculations adds layers to the already intricate mystery of Satoshi Nakamoto's identity. The diverse range of individuals and their varying backgrounds - from mathematicians and cryptographers to entrepreneurs and even criminal figures - underscores the widespread impact and appeal of Bitcoin, as well as the enduring fascination with the identity of its creator. The story of Nakamoto remains a captivating puzzle in the digital world, with each proposed theory contributing to the rich tapestry of ideas and conjectures surrounding the inception of the revolutionary cryptocurrency.

John Titor

In the waning days of 2000, an enigmatic figure emerged on the burgeoning digital landscape of the Internet, adopting the alias John Titor—or, as he initially introduced himself, "Time_Traveler_0". His first foray into the public eye was a post on a relatively obscure forum dedicated to time travel discussions, the Time Travel Institute Forum.

His opening message was simple yet intriguing: "Greetings. I am a time traveler from the year 2036. I am on my way home after retrieving an IBM 5100 computer system from the year 1975." This bold claim immediately captured the imagination of the forum's users. Titor elaborated that his journey included a detour to the year 2000 to collect old family photographs and visit relatives in Tampa and Rochester.

This remarkable introduction served as the catalyst for an intense and speculative four-month engagement with the online community. The forums, a nexus for paranormal, extraterrestrial, and conspiracy theory enthusiasts, became a buzzing hub of activity. Titor, through his numerous responses and postings, painted a vivid picture of his life in 2036, tantalizingly offering glimpses into what he claimed was our future.

In these posts, which numbered around 570, Titor outlined a series of foreboding predictions: a civil conflict in the United States sparked by a presidential election, an outbreak of Mad Cow Disease, and an ominous nuclear confrontation with Russia.

But on March 24, 2001, John Titor's voice fell silent. His final message, as he purportedly prepared to return to 2036, was a cryptic piece of advice: "Bring a gas can with you when the car dies on the side of the road. Farewell. John."

However, the disappearance of John Titor did not signify the end of his enigmatic legacy. In fact, it marked the beginning of an even larger cultural phenomenon. Those four months of interaction and the approximately 570 posts became the foundation for a growing mythos. This led to the creation of a dedicated website (JohnTitor.com), inspired a series of books (notably "John Titor: A Time Traveler's Tale"), a film adaptation ("Time Traveler Zero"), a stage play ("Time Traveler Zero Zero"), and even a video game ("Steins Gate").

The intrigue surrounding Titor's identity and claims spurred private investigations, legal battles, and a significant number of individuals who, for various reasons, chose to remain silent about their involvement or knowledge of the story. Thus, the John Titor phenomenon, far from fading into obscurity, continued to evolve and expand, leaving an indelible mark on the fabric of early internet culture and the world of science fiction and conspiracy theories.

In one of his early postings, John Titor shared intimate details about his life in the year 2036. He painted a picture of a post-apocalyptic existence in central Florida, where he lived with his family. Titor was not just any civilian survivor; he was a member of a specialized military unit, the 177th Temporal Recon Unit, based out of an Army base in Tampa. This unit's primary objective was to embark on time-travel missions to retrieve items crucial for the survival and rebuilding of society in 2036.

Titor's narrative was rich with personal and emotional details. He spoke of a world where the ravages of a civil war followed by a limited nuclear conflict with Russia had reshaped society. These catastrophic events had forged stronger bonds among the survivors. For Titor, life revolved around the family unit and the community at large. The thought of living even a few hundred miles away from his parents was inconceivable to him in that future world.

The mission that brought John Titor into the public eye in the year 2000 was a journey back to Rochester, Minnesota in 1975. His objective was to acquire a piece of technological history: the IBM 5100. Touted as one of the first portable computers, this device held significant importance for Titor's time. He revealed a personal connection to this mission, noting that his grandfather had been a part of the IBM 5100 development team.

The importance of the IBM 5100, according to Titor, lay in its ability to "debug various legacy code computer programs" essential in 2036. He hinted at a unique and simple feature in the 5100, a feature that IBM had allegedly not included in any subsequent desktop computers. This feature required specific adjustments, only possible with the expertise of a software engineer from 1975.

In 2003, an investigation into the John Titor story uncovered a significant connection with B.D., a former member of IBM's 5100 team in Rochester. Choosing to remain anonymous, B.D. emerged as a vital link in unraveling the technical claims made by Titor. His insights shed light on a peculiar feature of the IBM 5100, which Titor had alluded to as critical for resolving technological challenges in the year 2036.

This feature, as revealed by B.D., was an innovative interface between the assembly code around the computer's ROM exterior and a hidden 360 emulator. Developed discreetly, this feature marked a significant advancement in computing at the time, yet remained a closely guarded secret of IBM.

Initially, B.D. speculated whether John Titor might be an elaborate fabrication, possibly crafted by a former IBM colleague from the 1970s. However, after reviewing Titor's posts, B.D. concluded that the information was likely sourced from material available on the internet, dismissing the possibility of an inside job. He specifically noted that the use of the term "legacy code" in Titor's posts was not characteristic of the terminology used by his IBM team.

Not a fan of science fiction narratives like 'Star Trek', B.D. expressed skepticism about the Titor phenomenon, suspecting it might be a creative endeavor to pique public interest or cause a stir.

Years later, B.D. transitioned from his role at IBM to become a well-known business figure and respected resident in Rochester. Despite playing a pivotal role in the John Titor narrative, he preferred to maintain his anonymity, overwhelmed by the extensive attention and response he received as a peripheral figure in the story.

B.D.'s cautious stance is comprehensible, given the constant media spotlight he faced due to his association with the Titor saga. This unwanted fame resulted in a deluge of inquiries and theories from time travel enthusiasts and conspiracy theorists.

The initial reporting on the John Titor story in 2003 had an extraordinary impact, overwhelming server capacities of both the Rochester Magazine and the Post Bulletin due to massive web traffic. The story's compelling nature drew the attention of platforms like the paranormal-focused late-night radio show 'Coast to Coast AM' and the 'Weekly World News', known for its outlandish stories.

B.D. was not alone in his reticence to further discuss the Titor story. Morey Haber, an experienced IT professional, similarly shied away from the limelight. Both individuals' reluctance to engage with the ongoing Titor intrigue reflects the intense and sometimes intrusive fascination surrounding the story, highlighting the intricate and burdensome implications of being associated, even marginally, with a narrative that intertwines science fiction with reality.

In 2008 and 2009, the Italian TV show "Voyager" and the website Hoax Hunter independently embarked on investigations into the identity of John Titor. These inquiries involved hiring private investigators, staking out P.O. boxes, and geolocating IP addresses.

Both groups separately concluded that John Titor might be Morey Haber, the Chief Technology Officer at BeyondTrust, a company specializing in identity protection. Alternately, they suggested Titor could be one of Morey's brothers, Lawrence Haber, an entertainment lawyer based in Florida, or John Rick Haber, a computer scientist. Other theories posited that Titor could be one of their sons or another close family member.

Eventually, Morey Haber issued a statement denying any connection to John Titor: "I am not John Titor, nor do I know who he is or if he really exists. This alias has been bestowed upon me on the Internet by conspiracy theorists, 'fact finders,' and fanatics. It represents the most bizarre case of identity impersonation and accusations I have seen in my over 25 years in the security and information technology field," he declared.

Morey also noted that his identity had been falsely linked to John Titor by online threat actors, creating intense and complex challenges for him in the digital realm.

Lawrence Haber, another frequent suspect in the Titor mystery, remarked that his involvement with the Titor story brought him "fame, fear, new relation-ships, but never fortune." Despite his extensive career as an entertainment attorney, he admitted that the Titor case had garnered him more recognition and headaches than any other project he had undertaken.

Lawrence went on to express his uncertainty about the true identity of John Titor, stating, "I still don't know for sure who the time traveler from 2036 was. It's not me, it's not my son, nor is it my brother. I know only one person who claims to have been in direct contact with John. In the back of my mind, I've always wondered if this could all be true."

The speculation also included Joel Kostuch, who grew up in Rochester and now works in media production in Orlando. His background shared similarities with Titor's, and he was rumored to have connections to the Habers. Additionally, it was alleged that Kostuch had filed the trademark for John Titor merchandise. However, attempts to reach him for comment were unsuccessful.

Venturing into the world of John Titor on the internet can lead one down a bewildering rabbit hole, filled with a cast of intriguing and sometimes controversial characters.

Among these is Marlin Pohlman, a computer engineer who sought a patent for a time travel machine inspired by Titor's descriptions. Pohlman's story took a dark turn when he was later sentenced to six years in prison for drugging and assaulting four women.

Another figure is John Hughston, an amateur sleuth who dedicated significant effort to the Titor mystery. Hughston produced a 40-minute video where he scrutinized the "phrase usage" in Titor's posts, comparing them to those of his primary suspects in an attempt to uncover the truth behind the identity of John Titor.

Pamela Moore is yet another interesting personality in this saga. She claimed to have received a "secret song" from John Titor, a piece of music meant to authenticate anyone who might later claim to be Titor. Moore's revelations also hinted at a potentially intimate relationship with Titor, adding another layer of complexity to the already enigmatic tale.

For each individual connected to the Titor story who opts for silence, there is someone else who is more than willing to share their thoughts and theories. There are those who fervently hope for the authenticity of Titor's time travel claims, and others who remain open to the possibility, even if skeptically.

Mike Sauve, author of "Who Authored the John Titor Legend?", is one of those who reflect on the Titor phenomenon with a mixture of intrigue and skepticism. Sauve acknowledges that if John Titor's time travel story is not true, the creation and perpetuation of the legend is nonetheless an impressive feat, demanding considerable creativity and effort. He muses, "I have no hard evidence, only glimmers of this nature, but as a theory, the breaching of temporality would explain a lot of the anomalous activity in the world today."

The John Titor story is viewed by many as a mirror reflecting societal tendencies, particularly in the context of the internet's role in shaping and spreading conspiracy theories.

It's important to contextualize the era when Titor's story emerged. In 2000, internet access was limited compared to today, with only about 350 million people online globally. The internet experience was predominantly through 56K dial-up modems, and popular online content included simple animations like the Dancing Baby and the Hampster Dance. The idea of connecting with someone from a distant place like China over the internet had an almost otherworldly feel to it.

Jacob Desjarlais, a producer of the Crackpot Podcast, notes the unique aspect of the Titor story in the realm of conspiracy theories. "Titor was fascinating because he stuck around and talked to people. It was the first time any 'conspiracy theory,' was truly interactive," he observes.

Desjarlais also points out the enduring nature of the Titor narrative despite numerous efforts to debunk it. "We learned a serious lesson about the persistence of conspiracy. Even after several decades of debunking, reality checks, and investigations, Titor persists. And all it took was a little bit of insider knowledge about the 5100 computer model and declaring that timelines alter a little when you jump around."

The narrative surrounding John Titor is marked by a series of predictions, many of which failed to materialize. Despite some early coincidences that seemed to lend credence to his claims, the majority of Titor's forecasts did not come true.

Titor did hint at an event resembling a Mad Cow Disease outbreak prior to the limited cases that emerged in the U.S. in 2003. He also correctly predicted that no weapons of mass destruction would be found in Iraq in 2003 and that China would launch an astronaut into orbit the same year. These early predictions that seemed to align with actual events briefly stirred excitement and even fear among Titor's followers.

However, many of Titor's more significant predictions did not come to pass. He claimed that after 2004, there would be no official Olympics, yet they have continued to be held. He foretold of a civil war starting in the United States in 2004, escalating to a Waco-type event every month, but this did not occur. Titor also predicted a World War in 2015 involving a limited nuclear strike between the U.S. and Russia, resulting in nearly 3 million casualties, which also did not happen.

For Titor's most devoted believers, the failure of these predictions is explained through the concept of a "temporal divergence." According to Titor, his very act of traveling back in time created a new 'worldline', distinct from the one in which he originally lived. His presence and possibly his warnings were said to have caused changes in the future events of this new worldline. Titor elaborated that the longer he stayed in the past, the greater the divergence from his original timeline would become. This notion of temporal divergence serves as a catch-22 for time travelers and offers a convenient explanation for the inaccuracy of Titor's predictions within the framework of his own narrative.

The Elevator Game

The enigmatic and tragic story of Elisa Lam, whose last known appearance was captured in a chilling elevator video at the Cecil Hotel, continues to perplex and haunt many to this day. This footage, eerie and inexplicable, shows Lam in a state of distress, engaging in actions that defy clear explanation. Days after this unsettling recording, her body was discovered in a most unlikely and horrifying place: the hotel's water tank. The circumstances of her death and how she ended up in such a location remain shrouded in mystery, sparking endless speculation and theories.

Among the numerous hypotheses that have emerged, one particularly intriguing theory has captured the imagination of conspiracy theorists and paranormal enthusiasts alike. This theory revolves around an enigmatic urban legend known as the Elevator Game, or "The Elevator to Another World." This game, not for the faint-hearted, traces its roots to Korean and Japanese folklore and involves a complex ritual purported to alter the very fabric of reality. Though its precise origins are nebulous, with some suggesting its emergence in the early 2010s, the game has gained a sinister reputation, particularly in online communities.

The Elevator Game's allure and notoriety have been magnified through various online narratives and accounts, often blurring the lines between myth and reality. Tragically, its association with the mysterious demise of Elisa Lam has only fueled its infamy, leading many to wonder if this otherworldly ritual could hold the key to unraveling the perplexing puzzle of Lam's final moments.

As the debate continues, the Elevator Game remains a symbol of the human fascination with the unknown, and the Elisa Lam case a poignant reminder of the mysteries that can lurk in the shadows of our reality.

The Elevator Game, cloaked in layers of mystery and intrigue, requires meticulous adherence to its rules for those daring to play—and perhaps, survive. This game is not merely a pastime but a venture into the unknown, demanding at least one brave participant and an elevator in a building towering with at least 10 floors. The procedure is complex, each step pivotal in the journey to what some believe is another dimension.

Step 1 involves the initial foray into this enigmatic game. As a player, you enter the elevator, either alone or with another equally daring individual. It's crucial that no one else joins you during this process, as their presence could disrupt the delicate balance of the ritual. Exiting the elevator at any point other than the designated moments not only breaks the spell but also necessitates a complete restart of the entire sequence.

In Step 2, the game truly begins. Here, you navigate the elevator through a specific and non-random order of floors: first ascending to the 4th floor, then descending to the 2nd, climbing again to the 6th, dropping back to the 2nd, rising to the 10th, and finally, making a descent to the 5th floor. This pattern must be followed without deviation, and under no circumstances should you disembark at any of these floors, for each step is a critical part of the ritual.

Step 3 presents a chilling encounter. Upon reaching the 5th floor, you may come across a mysterious woman. This part of the game is fraught with peril, as any interaction or even accidental eye contact with her could have dire consequences, including the unsettling possibility of being trapped in a realm far from the familiar confines of our world.

Step 4 is where the game reaches its climax. From the 5th floor, you attempt to return to the 1st floor. If the elevator obediently descends, it's imperative to leave immediately upon arrival, avoiding any contact or conversation with anyone. However, if the elevator defies your command and ascends instead, it is said that you have been granted access to another world, a place beyond our understanding. Alternatively, in a moment of panic or realization, you might choose to cease the game by pressing the emergency button, calling for rescue and perhaps pondering the mysteries you might have unraveled.

Steeped in supernatural lore and urban legend, tantalizes with the promise of a journey to another world, a realm beyond the ordinary. According to those who believe in the game's otherworldly powers, the experience upon reaching this alternate dimension can be both eerie and surreal. Descriptions of this realm vary, with some suggesting a landscape shrouded in darkness, devoid of electricity, and eerily abandoned. Tales from those who claim to have ventured there include haunting visions, such as the sole sight of a distant red cross amidst an otherwise barren vista. Reports of disorientation and loss of consciousness are not uncommon among these narratives.

For those who venture into this mysterious world and then seek a return to the familiar, the game allegedly offers a method of escape. This return journey, however, is laden with its own set of precise and critical steps, each as important as the last.

The first step in the return process demands locating and boarding the same elevator used for the initial journey. This task may prove challenging in the strange and disorienting environment, but persistent searching is advised for success.

Once the original elevator is found, the second step involves replicating the initial sequence of floor visits: traveling to the 4th, then the 2nd, followed by the 6th, back down to the 2nd, up to the 10th, and finally the 5th floor. Adhering to this exact pattern is emphasized as crucial for a safe return.

The third step requires pressing the button for the 1st floor once the 5th floor is reached. This action is meant to initiate the journey back to the starting point.

In the fourth step, if the elevator begins to ascend instead of descending, it's advised to act quickly and press the button for any other floor before reaching the 10th floor to avert being pulled further into the unknown. Alternatively, as a safer option, one could press the emergency button, sit tight, and wait for rescue, hoping that claustrophobia is not an issue.

With these steps completed, those who embarked on this otherworldly adventure are said to safely return to their own world. This game, intertwined with the tragic and mysterious case of a young woman believed by some to have been a participant, continues to fuel speculation and intrigue, serving as a chilling reminder of the thin veil that may exist between our world and realms unknown.

The mysterious and tragic case of Elisa Lam continues to intrigue and baffle those who delve into its details. Lam was a guest at the Cecil Hotel in Los Angeles, a location with a dark history marked by numerous murders and suicides since its opening in 1927. The concern for Lam's wellbeing arose when her parents did not hear from her on the expected day of her checkout, prompting them to alert the authorities. This led to an intensive search, but the only significant clue uncovered was a disturbing video of Lam in the hotel's elevator.

The footage, which has since become infamous, shows Lam exhibiting unusual and erratic behavior. She is seen entering and exiting the elevator multiple times, gesturing as if speaking to an unseen person, pressing multiple elevator buttons in a seemingly frantic manner, and displaying what appears to be a paranoid awareness of her surroundings. Strangely, throughout this episode, the elevator remains stationary with its doors open. This bewildering behavior fueled speculation and theories, particularly after Lam's body was found in a water tank on the hotel's roof, naked and deceased.

The official autopsy conducted by the Los Angeles County Coroner's Office concluded that Lam likely died due to accidental drowning. However, the police noted that Lam had a history of bipolar disorder, leading them to suggest that her death might have been the tragic consequence of a mental health crisis.

Yet, this explanation did not satisfy everyone, particularly those who believe in the supernatural aspects of the Elevator Game. These individuals speculated that Lam might have been engaged in playing this eerie game, breaking its crucial rule of not interacting with the mysterious woman that players are warned about in Step 3. They theorized that this breach could have resulted in Lam being transported to another dimension, preventing her from returning alive to our world.

Despite these theories, there is no concrete evidence supporting the involvement of the Elevator Game in Lam's death. Both the Los Angeles Police Department and Elevator Game enthusiasts lack definitive proof to fully explain the circumstances surrounding the tragedy. This leaves room for continued speculation and investigation, with some holding out hope that new information might emerge, perhaps from Lam's personal belongings or computer, which could shed light on her mindset and actions. However, as it stands, the case remains shrouded in mystery, with neither the rational nor the supernatural explanations providing a fully satisfactory resolution to the perplexing and tragic fate of Elisa Lam.

Valor por Tamaulipas

The Facebook page "Valor por Tamaulipas" ("Courage for Tamaulipas"), emerged as a beacon of truth in the tumultuous landscape of Mexico's drug violence, particularly in the state of Tamaulipas. This page, born on January 1, 2012, from the inspiration drawn by its anonymous creator from similar websites, swiftly grew into a crucial source of real-time information on drug-related violence and risk situations in Tamaulipas. Its content, rich in messages and photos, offers a gritty, unfiltered view of crime scenes, capturing everything from law enforcement actions, images of alleged criminals and extortionists, to the eerie sights of abandoned vehicles by the roadside, roadblocks, arsons, and the clandestine operations of oil theft and drug trafficking.

The significance of "Valor por Tamaulipas" extends beyond mere reporting; it serves as a lifeline for residents in northern Mexico, particularly those in Tamaulipas. Amidst the high levels of drug-related activities, Facebook users frequently turn to this page for timely updates on shootouts, carjackings, and missing person reports. The page operates on the contributions of its vigilant internet community, with an administrator dedicated to almost round-the-clock updates throughout the week. This commitment to sharing real-time information stands in stark contrast to the cautious approach of mainstream Mexican media, which often downplays the extent of violence due to fears of criminal retribution.

This platform has thus emerged as a vital outlet for crime watchdogs and concerned citizens, filling a void left by censored or silenced media outlets. Despite the spotty and sometimes unreliable nature of its reports, as noted by crime journalist James Barger from InSight Crime, "Valor por Tamaulipas" remains often the sole source of news on the ground happenings. Its impact and reach are global, with a following that extends beyond Mexico to the United States and other countries, evidencing a widespread appreciation and support for its efforts in shedding light on the harsh realities of Tamaulipas.

By April 2013, the page had garnered over 210,000 likes on Facebook, while its Twitter handle had attracted around 24,400 followers.

Tamaulipas, a state in Mexico, has become a battleground for two powerful transnational criminal organizations: the Gulf Cartel and Los Zetas. These groups are locked in a fierce struggle for dominance over the lucrative smuggling routes along the Texas border, an area notorious for its role in human trafficking, arms smuggling, and international narcotics trade. The Gulf Cartel, with roots tracing back to the 1930s as a bootlegging gang, evolved into a major drug trafficking organization by the 1980s, as documented by the United States Department of State. In contrast, Los Zetas emerged in the late 1990s and early 2000s, originally formed by ex-Mexican Army soldiers. Initially hired as enforcers for the Gulf Cartel, Los Zetas eventually splintered, leading to a violent schism in early 2010. This fracture set off a wave of daily shootouts, kidnappings, and mass slayings across Tamaulipas and its neighboring states, plunging the region into chaos.

In the context of this turmoil, Mexico has been deemed one of the world's most perilous countries for journalists, especially those covering organized crime and drug trafficking. Since the turn of the millennium, close to 100 journalists have been either kidnapped or murdered, with many cases remaining unsolved and unprosecuted. This pervasive violence and direct targeting of the press have compelled many local media outlets to minimize their reporting on these issues. Consequently, the populace increasingly relies on social media platforms like Valor por Tamaulipas for timely updates on the precarious security situation. However, this shift to digital journalism is not without its own perils. In a chilling illustration of these risks, journalist and blogger María Elizabeth Macías Castro was brutally murdered by Los Zetas in September 2011 for her online reporting of their criminal activities. That same month, the violent reprisals extended to two Twitter users in Nuevo Laredo, Tamaulipas, who were killed for their online denunciations.

By January 2013, the state of Tamaulipas had reached a staggering homicide rate of 36 per 100,000 inhabitants, with kidnapping and extortion also rampant. This harrowing landscape paints a grim picture of a region caught in the throes of relentless violence and lawlessness, underscoring the critical need for unfiltered information channels amidst a climate of fear and censorship.

In June 2012, the Gulf Cartel allegedly launched a Facebook page named Anti Valor por Tamaulipas, aiming to undermine the efforts of Valor por Tamaulipas. This page was created as a direct response, criticizing the latter for spreading information that it claimed was harmful to the community. By early 2013, Anti Valor por Tamaulipas had gained about 11,244 likes on Facebook.

In a dramatic turn of events, an unidentified drug trafficking group in Ciudad Victoria, Tamaulipas, issued fliers offering a reward of 600,000 pesos (approximately US$46,000) for information leading to the whereabouts of the administrator of Valor por Tamaulipas or any of his family members. This bounty included his parents, siblings, children, and wife. The flier even listed a Tamaulipas area code phone number for tip-offs. The administrator's response was stoic and resolved; he expressed his commitment to his role as a citizen, thanked his page's contributors for their support, and vowed to continue reporting on crime, despite the risks to his life. Following the threat, he revealed that his family had moved to the United States for safety, and advised his followers to avoid using personal accounts when contributing to the page, to protect their identities. He suspected that either Los Zetas or corrupt state officials were behind this threat.

On February 20, 2013, a chilling video surfaced online, showing a man, alleged to be a collaborator of Valor por Tamaulipas, kneeling next to an armed, masked figure. The man, in a calm voice, warned against posting on the page, just before being shot in the head. The administrator of Valor por Tamaulipas refused to comment on the video's authenticity and did not recognize the victim. Reports suggested that the Gulf Cartel might be behind this video, but these claims remained unconfirmed.

In April 2013, Proceso magazine reported an alarming allegation from sources within the Tamaulipas Prosecutor's Office, claiming that state governor Egidio Torre Cantú sought to discredit and shut down Valor por Tamaulipas. The governor was reportedly concerned about the page's growing influence and its portrayal of criminal organizations controlling the state, overshadowing his governance.

On May 22, 2013, Valor por Tamaulipas shared another disturbing video, this time featuring a man and a woman being interrogated by supposed drug traffickers, demanding the page's closure and the administrator's identity revelation. Initially presented as the administrator's family, he later clarified that they were not related to him, suggesting they were either mistakenly targeted or chosen randomly by the criminal group. In a response to this incident, Valor por Tamaulipas addressed the Tamaulipas authorities, holding them accountable for a death caused by cardiac arrest following the couple's abduction and accusing them of colluding with the Los Zetas cartel.

In the early hours of April 1, 2013, users were met with a sudden and unexplained shutdown of the Facebook and Twitter accounts of Valor por Tamaulipas. This abrupt closure sparked immediate concern and speculation. Shortly after, a new page bearing the same name appeared, managed by different administrators who expressed their intent to carry on the legacy of the original page, despite being uncertain about the fate of the original administrator.

Amidst this uncertainty, a similar page called Responsabilidad por Tamaulipas ("Responsibility for Tamaulipas") suggested that the shutdown of Valor por Tamaulipas was a temporary measure, aimed at enhancing the page and safeguarding the administrator. They cautioned their followers against imposter sites claiming to be the original page.

About a week later, the original Valor por Tamaulipas page re-emerged. However, the administrator released a statement indicating his intention to permanently shut down the page after 8 days. On Facebook, he cited his inability to effectively manage the page under the circumstances. "Organized crime has won against me and my family, but not against society or the thousands of contributors who trusted and supported this page despite their fears," he expressed, acknowledging the support and trust he had received over the year. He concluded with an apology to his followers.

During the announced 8-day period, the page continued its usual operations. After much contemplation, the administrator ultimately decided to keep the page active, expressing gratitude for the overwhelming support from the media and followers. He acknowledged the uncertainty of whether continuing the page was beneficial or merely stubborn, but he felt honored to have worked with the community. "Thank you, people of goodwill from Tamaulipas. I owe it all to you," he said, affirming his commitment to the cause and the people he served.

On June 9, 2014, the Facebook page of Valor por Tamaulipas faced a one-month suspension due to the posting of content related to firearms, which violated Facebook's community standards. In response, the administrator shifted to using his Twitter and Google accounts to maintain the flow of information.

Tragically, on October 15, 2014, a grim incident shook the community associated with these pages. María del Rosario Fuentes Rubio, known by her Twitter handle @Miut3 and nickname Felina, and a former co-administrator of the sister page Responsabilidad por Tamaulipas, was kidnapped, tortured, and murdered by individuals suspected to be part of organized crime. Fuentes Rubio was an active and influential voice on Twitter, regularly posting about dangerous situations, shootouts, and the activities of criminal groups in Tamaulipas. Her captors reportedly used her Twitter account to post several chilling messages. The initial tweet revealed her identity and profession as a doctor, declaring an end to her life. Subsequent tweets advised against making the same mistakes she did in reporting on organized crime. Another tweet specifically warned Valor por Tamaulipas and other Twitter users about the risks of such posts. The final, harrowing tweet urged others to close their accounts to protect their families, accompanied by two photos: one showing her alive, and the other displaying her bloodied corpse. Despite Twitter's eventual deactivation of the account, these images had already spread widely on social media.

Valor por Tamaulipas confirmed her death on its Facebook page, expressing sorrow over the tragic event. The page acknowledged that @Miut3 was not only a collaborator at Valor por Tamaulipas but also a former administrator at Responsabilidad por Tamaulipas. While the precise motive for her murder remained unclear, with speculation about whether it was linked to her social media activities or her medical profession, Valor por Tamaulipas cast doubt on one theory that suggested her kidnapping was a retaliation for the death of a drug lord's son due to medical complications. The administrator of Valor por Tamaulipas expressed a belief that her targeted killing was due to her online activism. Furthermore, the page noted that @Miut3 had received threats from another Twitter user, @garzalaura142, just a week prior to her murder, suggesting a connection in the language used in these threats and her subsequent killing.

On November 29, 2014, a significant announcement was made on Facebook by the administrator of Valor por Tamaulipas. He declared his decision to step down from his role, citing personal reasons. Despite his departure, he assured that the page would continue its operations under new leadership. Intriguingly, he mentioned that the incoming administrator had connections to law enforcement, a detail he believed would be advantageous for the online community. This link would potentially enable direct communication between citizen reporters and law enforcement authorities.

In addition to the changes at Valor por Tamaulipas, the administrator announced that other related pages, namely Responsabilidad, Fortaleza, and Valor por la Huasteca, would also transition to new management. He expressed confidence in the new team, chosen for their trustworthiness, either due to their long-standing support or personal losses suffered due to the ongoing violence.

In his farewell message, the outgoing administrator expressed gratitude towards God for the joy brought into his life, both personally and professionally. The comments section of the Facebook post reflected a mix of emotions from the page's followers. Many expressed their appreciation for the administrator's efforts and support over the years. However, there were also voices of concern regarding the new management, particularly due to its ties with the government, reflecting a sense of apprehension about the future direction and integrity of the page under this new leadership.

Conclusion

I n the digital realm of internet mysteries, a peculiar crossroads of knowledge and enigma emerges. This journey, akin to a roller coaster, spirals through tales of intrigue, puzzles, and unexplained phenomena lurking in the vast, uncharted territories of the internet.

Each unraveling mystery is a unique story, a distinct piece of an immense puzzle. From the perplexing conundrums of Cicada 3301 to the eerie echoes of Webdriver Torso, these tales venture into realms where reality blurs with fiction, and facts intertwine with myths. Despite their differences, they share a common thread: they are a testament to the boundless curiosity and ingenuity of netizens worldwide.

A profound lesson from these mysteries is the incredible power of collective effort. The internet, in all its complexity, is a network of minds. It is a platform where collective intelligence can unravel intricate enigmas, as seen in the collaborative efforts to solve puzzles like Cicada 3301. This synergy, transcending geographical and cultural barriers, embodies the true spirit of the internet – a tool for unification and discovery.

However, the exploration of these mysteries also reveals the internet's darker facets. It can be a double-edged sword – a haven for creative expression and knowledge-sharing, yet also a breeding ground for hoaxes, misinformation, and digital folklore. The tales of Chip-chan and the mystique of John Titor are stark reminders of how easily fiction can be woven into the fabric of internet reality, often leaving a permanent imprint on digital culture.

These stories highlight the fluid nature of truth in the digital age. In a realm where information can be manipulated and digital footprints can be fabricated, the line between fact and fiction becomes increasingly blurred. It prompts discernment and critical thinking in the digital wilderness.

Looking ahead, the future of internet mysteries is as enigmatic as the puzzles themselves. The rapid evolution of technology, with advancements in artificial intelligence, virtual reality, and blockchain, opens new doors for mysteries. The internet, as a living entity, will continue to evolve, and with it, the nature and complexity of its mysteries.

In essence, the world of internet mysteries is a celebration of the human quest for knowledge and understanding. It is a tribute to curious minds that refuse to accept the mundane, seeking to peer beyond the veil of the ordinary. The internet mysteries explored are not just puzzles; they are mirrors reflecting collective curiosity, creativity, and an unquenchable thirst for the unknown.

In conclusion, the realm of internet mysteries is a tapestry woven with curiosity, creativity, and caution. It continuously challenges perceptions and urges exploration and connection. It is a realm guided by wisdom, enriched by discovery, and illuminated by understanding. The internet is a map, a treasure chest, and an enigma, with its mysteries waiting to be unraveled by the daring, the curious, and the vigilant.

The next mystery is just a click away. Continuing to explore, question, and maintain the flame of curiosity is vital. The mysteries of the internet are not just stories; they are invitations to embark on a journey of discovery – a journey endlessly fascinating, perpetually evolving, and eternally mysterious.

Bibliography

Wehner, Mike, "The creepy puzzle video just keeps getting creepier", Daily Dot, 21 Oct 2015, https://www.dailydot.com/debug/creepy-puzzle-video-poland-11b-x-1371/

Krahbichler, Johny, "Part Two Of The Creepy Puzzle '11B 3 1369'", GadgetZZ, n.d., https://gadgetzz.com/2016/01/01/part-two-of-the-creepy-puzzle-11b-3-1369/

Kushner, David (29 January 2015). "Cicada: Solving the Web's Deepest Mystery". No. 1227. Rolling Stone.

Bell, Chris, "The internet mystery that has the world baffled", The Telegraph, 25 November 2013, https://www.telegraph.co.uk/technology/internet/10468112/The-internet-mystery-that-has-the-world-baffled.html

Browne, David, "The Unsolved Case of the Most Mysterious Song on the Internet", Rolling Stone, 24 September 2019, https://www.rollingstone.com/music/music-features/most-mysterious-song-on-the-internet-885106/

Jones, Alexandra Mae, "Help solve a decades-long mystery: What is the name of this mysterious 80s song?" CTV News, 18 November 2019, https://www.ctvnews.ca/entertainment/help-solve-a-decades-long-mystery-what-is-the-name-of-this-mysterious-80s-song-1.4690967

Dewey, Caitlin, "Five of the Internet's eeriest, unsolved mysteries", The Washington Post, 2 May 2014, https://www.washingtonpost.com/news/arts-and-entertainment/wp/2014/05/02/five-of-the-internets-eeriest-unsolved-mysteries/

Staff, Buzzfeed, "There's A Game That's Surfaced From The Deep Web And It's Scary As Hell", Buzzfeed, 7 Oct 2015, https://www.buzzfeed.com/bfstaff/sleep-tight-ghost-babies

Shilling, Eric, "The Unsettling Mystery of the Creepiest Channel on

YouTube", Atlas Obscura, 22 February 2016, https://www.atlasobscura.com/articles/the-unsettling-mystery-of-the-creepiest-channel-on-youtube

Wakefield, Jane, "Google behind Webdriver Torso mystery", BBC, 10 June, 2014, https://www.bbc.com/news/technology-27778071

Tucker, Teagan, "Chip Chan: The Internet's Most Bizarre Live Streamer", Medium, n.d., https://medium.com/@teagantucker/chip-chan-the-internets-most-bizarre-live-streamer-f53587b488f9

Reed, Betsy, "China accused over global computer spy ring", The Guardian, n.d., https://www.theguardian.com/world/2009/mar/30/china-dalai-lama-spying-computers

Biggs, John, "Who Is The Real Satoshi Nakamoto? One Researcher May Have Found The Answer", Tech Crunch, 5 December 2013, https://techcrunch.com/2013/12/05/who-is-the-real-satoshi-nakamoto-one-researcher-may-have-found-the-answer/

Unknown, "Time travel paradoxes!", Time Travel Institute, 23 October 2000, https://timetravelinstitute.com/threads/time-travel-paradoxes.943/